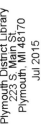
j292.13S

CB
6/15

HEROES AND LEGENDS

JASON
AND THE ARGONAUTS

BY NEIL SMITH
ILLUSTRATED BY JOSÉ DANIEL CABRERA PEÑA

ROSEN
PUBLISHING

NEW YORK

Published in 2015 by The Rosen Publishing Group, Inc.
29 East 21st Street, New York, NY 10010

© 2015 Osprey Publishing Limited
First published in paperback by Osprey Publishing Limited
All rights reserved

First Edition

Library of Congress Cataloging-in-Publication Data
Smith, Neil (Historian)
 Jason and the Argonauts/Neil Smith.
    pages cm. — (Heroes and legends)
 Includes bibliographical references and index.
 ISBN 978-1-4777-8138-8 (library bound)
 1. Jason (Greek mythology)—Juvenile literature. 2. Argonauts (Greek mythology)—Juvenile
literature. I. Title.
 BL820.A8S65 2015
 398.20938'02)—dc23
                                                                                2014020515

Manufactured in the United States of America

Contents

INTRODUCTION

The story of Jason and the Argonauts, and their search for the Golden Fleece, is one of the oldest in the western canon. As such, it sits beside Homer's *Iliad* and *Odyssey* as one of our few non-archaeological insights into the world of Bronze Age Greece. At its most basic level, the story tells of a voyage of exploration from Iolcus in Greece along the Black Sea to the kingdom of Aeëtes, in the vicinity of modern-day Georgia.

The journey probably took place around 1300 BCE, before the wars with Troy described by Homer. As with Homer's epics, though, the retelling of events through the ages introduced contemporary ideas and values into the original story, creating a fog of information that has taken sophisticated scholarship to penetrate. Even with all that work, many mysteries remain, and debate continues over the major issues of myth and history, cultural interpolation, and the meaning of the story.

Jason's story began life as an oral history passed down through the generations. The most complete written version that has survived was recorded by the Hellenistic scholar Apollonius of Rhodes in the first half of the third-century BCE. He worked at the library of Alexandria and infused the story of Jason with the latest cultural and scholarly knowledge. Apollonius's literary inspiration probably came from the fifth-century Theban poet Pindar, who wrote a brief account of Jason's voyage in his fourth Pythian ode. It would be another three hundred years before an updated version of the Jason myth would again be written, this time by a Roman, Gaius Valerius Flaccus.

As with Apollonius, little is now known about Valerius Flaccus. He lived in the first century CE in the town of Setia, south of Rome, and may have been reasonably prominent among his contemporaries. His only existing work, however, is the incomplete *Argonautica*. Flaccus based the style of his poetic version on Virgil's *Aeneid*, but his epic was not of the same quality. Nevertheless, Flaccus's version of the myth added significant new elements to the story and opened up debates over the characters involved, especially the hero of the story and his relationship to both his crew and Medea. With two versions available to them, literary historians have embarked on their own voyage into the nature of the epic poem, and how the story has been told through the ages.

Various modern translations of Apollonius and Valerius Flaccus have been attempted, along with two big movie productions and a video game. While they differ in intent and accuracy, texts and movies point to a continued fascination with the story of Jason, his hunt for the legendary Golden Fleece, and his dramatic love affair with the enigmatic princess—and sorceress—Medea.

At its heart, the *Argonautica* is a quest story that sets the narrative foundation for future great adventures, such as the medieval Grail-quest romances of King Arthur and Tolkien's *Lord of the Rings* in the twentieth century. They are all stories in which men and women interact with supernatural forces while undergoing a series of trials on their way to recover a mystical object; monsters stalk the adventurers and some die along the way; heroes rise and fall according to circumstance, and romance is never far away.

Somewhere along the path, through the mists of time, and amid intense scholarly analysis, the incredible story of Jason and his intrepid crew has become complicated in many ways. We no longer believe in the gods of the Greeks, for example, and reconstructions of the quest are rationalized on the basis of modern knowledge. Some analysts are more focused on literary aspects, and movies have their own agendas to pursue. This version of the tale presents the *Argonautica* without judgement or prejudice, as a straightforward story for the enjoyment of the reader, compiled from the various translations—most notably those of Apollonius, with the assistance of Valerius Flaccus.

A seventeenth-century map illustrating the regions through which Jason and the Argonauts travelled.

5

Book I: The Journey Begins

The Man with One Sandal

The story of how Jason and his Argonauts retrieved the Golden Fleece begins in the small kingdom of Iolcus in eastern Greece. It was here that Pelias usurped the throne from his half-brother, Aeson, in a ruthless coup, and launched a reign of terror. An oracle had warned the new king that he would die at the hands of a descendant of Aeolus, the ruler of the winds. Pelias therefore set about killing every Aeolian he could lay hands on, but spared Aeson for the sake of their mother. Aeson instead had to renounce his inheritance and remain a prisoner in Pelias's palace. The king's mercy did not extend to any child of Aeson's, however; so when Aeson's wife gave birth to a son, she and her midwives pretended that the newborn did not survive childbirth. He was then smuggled out of the city to the safety of Mount Pelion where Cheiron the Centaur raised him as Jason. On reaching manhood, at the age of twenty, Jason set off for Iolcus to recover his rightful inheritance. Cheiron wished him well and waved goodbye, and, with that, Jason walked off to find his destiny.

The Education of Achilles by James Barry. Cheiron the Centaur served as a tutor and surrogate father to many of the heroes of Ancient Greece, including Jason.

A second oracle had cautioned Pelias that the man prophesied to kill him would arrive while wearing only one sandal. Years passed but no one fitting that unusual description came to Iolcus, and the king got on with the business of ruling his kingdom. One of the most important functions of Greek rulers was to honor the gods through regular devotions, feasts, and games. Pelias also had a personal reason to do so, as his father was Poseidon, god of the sea. Conversely, dishonoring the gods could result in dire consequences, especially for kings.

In Pelias's case, he had once offended the goddess Hera, the wife of the all-powerful Zeus, by killing his stepmother in Hera's temple. When, one day well into his reign, Pelias organized an Olympiad in honor of Poseidon, Hera seized her chance. If her plan worked, the prophecy would come true and the goddess would have her revenge.

The Golden Fleece

The story of the Golden Fleece originated in the generation before Jason launched his epic voyage. It was then that the king of Boeotia, Athamas, had an affair with Ino while still married to his queen Nephele. The queen was furious to be supplanted by Ino but there was little she could do other than rant about the travesty. In the meantime, Ino plotted to destroy Nephele's children, Phrixus and Helle, so that her sons by Athamas—Learches and Melicertes—would inherit the kingdom. To that end, Ino had tainted corn seed sown for the next growing season, resulting in a complete crop failure. Athamas, as predicted by Ino, consulted the Delphic Oracle to find a solution, but Ino bribed the king's messengers to bring back instructions that Athamas was to sacrifice Phrixus if he wanted the crops to grow again. Although devastated, the king had no option but to oblige.

On hearing of this hideous bargain, Zeus ordered the god Hermes to send a winged, golden ram to rescue Phrixus and carry him off to Colchis where he would be safe. Phrixus's sister, Helle, jumped on board too but fell off into the sea, giving her name to the Hellespont strait that separates Asia and Europe. On his arrival

in Colchis, well out of the reach of the Greeks—or so he believed—Phrixus sacrificed the ram to Zeus and gave the Fleece to King Aeëtes of Colchis for safekeeping. Aeëtes placed the Fleece in a tree where it lay under the protection of a great serpent.

Phrixus riding the golden ram.
(Stefano Bolognini)

Jason had come to the River Anaurus, which was his last obstacle before reaching Iolcus. As he was about to wade across, he saw a small old woman on his side of the river, who could not get over on her own. Jason offered to carry her across, and she duly accepted. Jason was stunned at how heavy the woman was, not knowing he carried Hera in disguise, and he staggered, losing his sandal in the process. With this part of her scheme accomplished, Hera climbed down on to dry land, and promptly vanished. A bemused Jason looked round for the woman, and his sandal, but he had no time to waste on such small mysteries. Jason gathered himself and carried on down the road.

King Pelias was still at his Olympiad when the one-sandaled man walked in, but if he felt any surprise, he hid it well. Rather, he invited the young man to the evening feast. There he asked the newcomer his name and parentage, or origin. "Jason, formerly Diomedes, son of Aeson," replied the intruder. Pelias followed up quickly, asking Jason what he would do if an oracle warned that a citizen was going to kill him. Jason took the bait, replying that he would send the threatening man on a quest to fetch the Golden Fleece from Colchis, knowing that he would never return from such a hazardous mission. Pelias now revealed his identity to his uninvited guest. Jason countered by declaring his ancestry, and told Pelias that he was here to take back his rightful inheritance. The king sprung his trap, telling Jason that the land was cursed and only by retrieving the Golden Fleece could it prosper once more; if Jason made it back with the Fleece, however, Pelias would abdicate.

Jason had left himself two choices: accept the mission, or withdraw in humiliation from the challenge. The epic quest for the Golden Fleece was about to begin.

The **Argo**

The news that an daring attempt to recover the Golden Fleece was about to get underway flashed like wildfire through the Greek world, energizing men and gods alike. Of the latter, Hera's interest was already engaged through Pelias's disrespect, and it was she who put the thought of taking the challenge into Jason's head when Pelias dropped his loaded question at the feast. Jason also appealed to Pallas Athena, goddess of wisdom and courage, to add her inspiration and support to the expedition. In return, he promised to adorn her temple with the recaptured Fleece. Athena heard Jason's prayer and whispered into the mind of the master boatbuilder Argus that he must create the ship to carry Jason and his men—the ship would be named the *Argo* in his honor. For her part, Hera helped spread the word of the quest, making sure the best possible men would assemble to form Jason's crew.

Hera, queen of the gods and Jason's strongest ally in Olympus. (Farnese Collection)

THE *ARGO* CREW LIST

The crew list for the *Argo* reads like a who's who of legendary Greek characters, many of whom were directly connected to, and even sons of, the gods. It includes:

Acastus: Son of the usurper who seized the throne, Pelias.

Admetus: king of Pherae.

Aethalides: Son of the god Hermes, could remember everything.

Amphidamas: From Arcadia, son of Aleus.

Amphion: Son of Hyperasius.

Ancaeus: From Arcadia, arrived wearing a bearskin and carrying a great double-edged axe.

Ancaeus: From Parthenia, son of Poseidon.

Areius: From Argus, son of Pero.

Argus: Builder of the *Argo*.

Asterion: Brother of Amphion.

Atalanta: The only woman on the quest, she had been raised by bears and fought like one.

Augeas: king of the Eleans, brother of Aeëtes of Colchis.

Butes: Son of noble Teleon.

Calaïs: Winged son of the god Boreas.

Canthus: From Euboea but would never return from the quest.

Castor: From Sparta, brother of Polydeuces.

Cepheus: Brother of Amphidamas.

Clytius: Son of cruel Eurytus.

Coronus: A brave man from Gyrton in Thessaly.

Echion: Son of Hermes, brother of Erytus.

Erginus: Brother of Ancaeus, son of Poseidon.

Eribotes: Son of Teleon.

Erytus: Brother of Echion.

Euphemus: Son of Poseidon who could run across water.

Eurydamas: Son of Ctimenus.

Eurytion: Son of Irus.

Heracles: The legendary hero.

Hylas: Youthful squire to Heracles.

Idas: Brother of Lynceus.

Idmon: Seer who knew he would die on the journey but came anyway.

Iphicles: Arrived with Meleager, and an expert with javelin and in hand-to-hand fighting.

Iphitos: Brother of Clytius.

Iphitus: Jason's maternal uncle.

Laërtes: Father of Odysseus.

Laocoön: Sent to act as a guide for Meleager.

Leodocus: From Argos, son of Pero.

Lynceus: Possessed extraordinary eyesight, brother of Idas.

Meleager: Leader of the famous hunt for the Calydonian boar.

Menoetius: Son of Actor, father of Patroclus.

Mopsus: Prophet who understood the language of birds.

Nauplius: Descendant of Danaus.

Oileus: Skilled at pursuing a broken enemy.

Orpheus: His songs could charm the mountains and rivers.

Palaemonius: Crippled in both feet, like his father, Hephaestus, but not lacking in courage.

Peleus: From Phthia; exiled son of Aeacus, and father of Achilles.

Periclymenus: Son of Neleus, who could transform into various animals.

Phalerus: The Athenian who carried an ashen spear.

Phlias: Son of Dionysus.

Polydeuces: Brother of Castor, skilled with horses.

Polyphemus: A veteran of the war against the Centaurs.

Talaus: From Argos, son of Pero.

Telamon: From Attica, brother of Peleus and also exiled.

Tiphys: The expert navigator, sent by Athena.

Zetes: Brother of Calaïs, also a winged warrior.

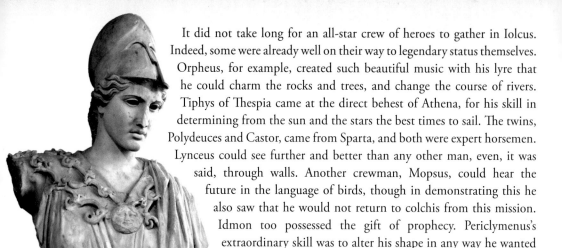

It did not take long for an all-star crew of heroes to gather in Iolcus. Indeed, some were already well on their way to legendary status themselves. Orpheus, for example, created such beautiful music with his lyre that he could charm the rocks and trees, and change the course of rivers. Tiphys of Thespia came at the direct behest of Athena, for his skill in determining from the sun and the stars the best times to sail. The twins, Polydeuces and Castor, came from Sparta, and both were expert horsemen. Lynceus could see further and better than any other man, even, it was said, through walls. Another crewman, Mopsus, could hear the future in the language of birds, though in demonstrating this he also saw that he would not return to colchis from this mission. Idmon too possessed the gift of prophecy. Periclymenus's extraordinary skill was to alter his shape in any way he wanted during combat. Zetes and Calaïs, sons of Boreas, had wings and could fly. Polyphemus had fought against centaurs long before this voyage, and was still a formidable warrior. Jason's uncle, Iphitus, came along as part of his familial obligations. Hermes's cunning sons Erytus and Echion arrived on hearing the call. Ancaeus reached Iolcus dressed in a bearskin and brought with him a monstrous two-handed battleaxe. Atalanta the huntress joined the crew to become the only woman in the ship's company. Greece's mightiest warrior Heracles heard of the impending adventure while in the middle of his legendary twelve labors. He dropped everything to travel to Iolcus, bringing with him his young weapon carrier, Hylas. Argus the shipbuilder would not stay behind while his creation sailed, and, finally, Acastus, the son of King Pelias, joined in, much to the shock and annoyance of his father. Collectively, the locals called the crew the Minyans for their association with Minyas, who had founded Boeotia; they became known to history and legend as the Argonauts.

Athena, goddess of wisdom and war, also proved a strong supporter of Jason and the Argonauts during their quest. (Found *c.* 1770 in Tusculum in the Villa of Licinius Murena/ Vitold Muratov)

The Quest Begins

While the crewmembers arrived in ones and twos, Argus had got on with the job of building and provisioning his ship. When all was ready, the Argonauts gathered in the city to march down to the beach, where the *Argo* now waited for her launching. In a scene reminiscent of men going off to risk their lives throughout history, the people of Iolcus crowded round, the women noisily exhorting the gods to watch over the intrepid adventurers.

One of those most affected was Jason's mother, Alcimede. As he prepared to leave her house, she clung to Jason in sorrow and regret that he should be the one to make the attempt on the Golden Fleece. Jason told her not to grieve, because that might prove an ill omen. He added that the gods would look after him and the Argonauts, and that the oracles were in their favor. Untangling himself from his mother's embrace, Jason left her to take his place on the beach.

Athena helps Argus and Jason to build the *Argo*. (Marie-Lan Nguyen/Wikimedia Commons)

When the tumult died down and crowds had dispersed, the Argonauts stood together on the beach, beside the sail and the mast. Jason asked them all to sit, and announced that, as they would be sailing soon, it was time to elect a leader. There was only one candidate for most of the Argonauts and they chanted his name: Heracles. The great man of legend would hear none of it, however, and hushed the furor with an outstretched hand. Not only would he not accept the captaincy of the expedition, he refused to even hear the matter debated. As far as he was concerned there was only one captain, and that was Jason. The Argonauts nodded their assent, then Jason rose to speak. His first orders were for the crew to drag the ship down to the sea and finish gathering provisions. In the meantime, they were to prepare a feast and sacrifice two bulls to honor the god Apollo, who, through an oracle, had promised to show them the way across the sea. With that, Jason turned to the work at hand, getting the ship ready for launch.

The need for teamwork in this quest for the Golden Fleece was not reserved for those moments of glory where legends are made. Even the most seemingly mundane tasks needed many hands, and so the Argonauts had to come together immediately just to get their ship into the water. Argus took charge of this operation. They first strengthened the ship by stretching a rope down the sides, and then dug a trench down the beach, as wide as the hull. The crew next placed polished rollers into the trench and readied themselves to push the boat over the rollers and into the sea. When they were in position, Tiphys jumped on board to direct the launch. At his signal, the crew pushed with all their might, starting the *Argo* on its path. Once the ship had started

to move, their task was to slow it down by pulling on the oars to keep it on a steady track. In that manner, the *Argo* slid into the sea, where her Argonauts fitted the oars and mast, and anchored the vessel.

Satisfied once the *Argo* was safely secured, the Argonauts drew lots to determine their seating. The benches on either side of the ship each sat two, but the middle seats were assigned to Heracles and Ancaeus, who were the largest and strongest men. The Argonauts unanimously elected Tiphys to steer. With that done, it was now time to honor Apollo with prayer and celebration. The crew raised an altar, using the shingle from the beach, and placed logs of dried olive wood on top.

While that was going on, two bulls were brought down to the beach, along with barley meal and lustral water. Jason saw that everything was in order, and stepped forward to exhort Apollo to guide the voyage and raise soft breezes to speed them on their way. He cast the barley meal, then Ancaeus and Heracles each brought down a steer with a single blow. The rest of the crew carved up the bulls, removing the thigh bones so they could be covered in fat and placed on the altar. Jason lit the sacrifice, with Idmon, beside him, paying close attention to the omens in the smoke. The omens were good, Idmon said; the crew would return with the Golden Fleece, but he, Idmon—like Mopsus—would not, as he was destined to die during the journey.

With dusk falling, the Argonauts spread leaves on the beach to sit on while they ate their feast, drank wine, and talked. Their banter and boasting soon grew lively but Jason sat alone to one side, lost in thought. One of the men, Idas, noticed Jason, and called out to him that he need not be afraid, because

The *Argo* departs Iolcus. (North Wind Picture Archives/Alamy)

no venture failed with Idas as part of the team. He then greedily gulped down a full goblet of wine to the acclaim of some of the crew—but not Idmon, who reminded Idas what happens to those who would taunt the gods with bold prophecies. Idas, having none of it, retorted that if Idmon was so good at prophecy, then what was in store for him? Then two men shaped up to fight and the crew began to take sides, ignoring Jason's urging that they stop. It was the musician Orpheus who had the last say in the matter. He raised his lyre and began to sing a song of the heavens and the sea, of mountains and rivers, and of how they all came to be. The Argonauts fell into silence, enchanted by the beautiful and soothing song even after Orpheus had stopped playing. The argument and the feast were over, and the Argonauts went to sleep on the beach, after saying a brief prayer to Zeus.

Tiphys woke first, just after dawn, and roused the rest of the Argonauts: it was time to set sail. The crew took their places, stowing their armor and weapons under the benches, where they could reach them easily in a crisis. The men at the back cast off the ropes that tied the *Argo* to the beach while others offered a brief sacrifice of wine to Poseidon. As for Jason, he would not look back, but only forward. He gave the signal; Orpheus began to pluck on his lyre, Tiphys grabbed the helm to steer, and the crew, as one, dipped their oars into the water and heaved. Smoothly, the ship sped out towards the harbor entrance. Once out into the deeper water, the Argonauts mounted the mast in its box and secured it with forestays, a type of rigging that holds the mast up. They next unfurled the large, square sail, which immediately caught the breeze and billowed out, pulling the ship past the headland and out into the sea.

(Overleaf) A Gathering of Heroes. This image depicts all of the Argonauts gathering before they set off in the *Argo*. The exact crew of the *Argo* changes with nearly every telling of the tale. While some heroes, such as Heracles, Orpheus, Polydeuces and the Boreads appear in every version, others only appear in some. For example, Atalanta appears in most versions, but Apollonius says Jason would not take a woman on the quest. Other Greek heroes, such as Theseus and Bellerophon, are also sometimes included among the Argonauts.

Jason

Heracles

Hylas

Ancaeus
the bearskin warrior

Erytus and Echion

Idas and Lynceus

Castor and Polydeuces
the Dioscuri

Laërtes
father of Odysseus

Idmon
the seer

Polyphemus

Orpheus
the musician

Tiphys
the navigator

Argus
the shipbuilder

Periclymenus
the metamorph

Zetes and Calaïs
the Boreads

Atalanta

Acastus
son of Pelias

Meleager
the calydonian Boar hunter

Telamon
father of Ajax

Mopsus

Peleus
father of Achilles

Into the Storm

The first day's sailing went well, and it was a satisfied Jason and crew that beached the ship at dusk beside the tomb of Dolops. The wind was beginning to turn, however, and the Argonauts found themselves stuck for two days with little to do but sacrifice some sheep to honor Dolops, and watch the anchored *Argo* ride the heavy swell. On the third morning, the wind changed directions again, and the eager Argonauts set sail once more. So far, the great adventure had proven very uneventful, but that was about to change.

Boreas, god of the north wind, saw the square-sailed *Argo* plowing its way through the sea and grew angry over the audacity of Jason and his band of heroes in challenging his power. He gathered all his strength, drawing in the wind from all directions to unleash on the disobedient ship. The first inklings the Argonauts had of Boreas's wrath was when the sky turned black as night and the waves began to rise. Then the wind struck. Boreas's fury ripped the oars from the sailors' hands, and twisted the ship's head around so that the *Argo* turned sideways into the storm. Boreas tore the sail from its mast and dipped the yardarm, part of what sustains the mast, into the water, much to the horror of the crewmen, many of whom now thought their last moments had arrived.

Worse was to come, however, as the south, west, and east winds joined in with Boreas to toss the *Argo* around like a child's toy. The ship's hull breached and began to break apart and water poured in over the sides. Then, just when

While it is impossible to determine the exact route of the *Argo*, this map gives a best guess based primarily on the text of Apollonius. Over the years, many different routes have been theorized, including one that has the Argonauts going all of the way across mainland Europe, out into the Atlantic Ocean and back into the Mediterranean Sea through the Straits of Gibraltar.

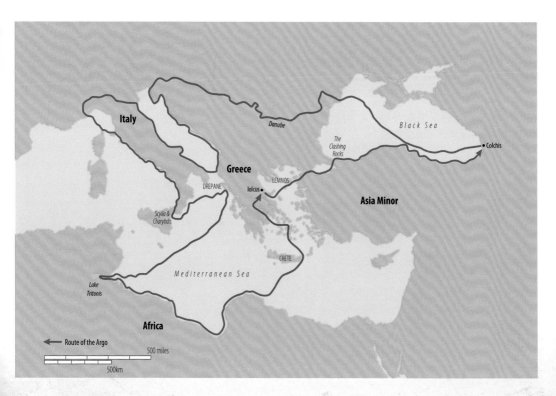

it seemed that Jason's quest was about to reach a sudden and dramatic end, Poseidon himself rose up in a fury of his own, having been urged to protect the *Argo* by Athena and Hera. He immediately calmed the sea and sent the storm rushing off to the south. The relieved Argonauts were saved, but also reminded once again of the power of their gods.

Interlude on Lemnos

The rejuvenated Argonauts sailed on, with favorable winds billowing out the broad sail and pushing the *Argo* along. Past Meliboea they cruised, then Olympus, home of the gods; they cleared the headland of Canastra at night, and, as dawn broke, the *Argo* was well on its way to the isle of Lemnos. The breeze stayed fresh all that day, before dying down towards evening, leaving the crew to row the final leg into Lemnos harbor. Once in port, Jason sent Aethalides to the queen of Lemnos, Hypsipyle, to ask her permission to come ashore. The impending visit of the Argonauts created a unique crisis on the island, however, because the inhabitants were all women and they hid a dark secret.

Sometime before the arrival of the *Argo*, the Lemnian women killed all the men on the island except one. The reason they did so was because the women were fed up with their men rejecting them, due to a curse imposed by Aphrodite, in favor of captive women brought home from their frequent raids. That sense of neglect grew into murderous rage until one night, the wives killed their husbands, the captives, and anyone on the island who might seek revenge. The one exception was the aging king of Lemnos, Thoas, whose daughter Hypsipyle threw him into an empty wooden chest and cast him adrift to suffer whatever fate had in store. Fortunately for the king, a passing fishing boat picked him up and dropped him off on the shore of the island of Oenoe.

After carrying out their grim deed, the Lemnian women took fright at the thought of Thracians arriving and asking about their men, the consequences of which could prove terrible. When they spotted the *Argo*'s sail, the Lemnian women therefore donned their husbands' armor, and ran down to the beach. There they met the friendly Aethalides much to their relief, but they still had the dilemma of the Argonauts finding out what they had done, so they withdrew to the city to discuss their options.

Hypsipyle opened the assembly. She wanted to provide the Argonauts with food and wine so that they would sail on without asking too many awkward questions. The queen's elderly nurse and seeress, Polyxo, foresaw a different problem from newly arrived warriors and their curiosity. By all means, she said, give the Argonauts food and wine, and, if they were lucky, their crimes would go unnoticed. But what would happen, she continued, when the women grew old and could neither defend themselves nor take care of the land? The answer was to trust the strangers and take them in as potential new husbands. The assembly agreed with Polyxo, urging Hypsipyle to send a messenger down to the ship and invite the Argonauts into the city.

The invitation delighted Jason and his crew, who got ready to leave the ship. Jason dressed for the occasion in a stunning purple cloak, given to him by the goddess Athena, which was richly embroidered with mythological scenes. He also picked up the spear given to him by Atalanta when she joined the crew. Jason then walked into the city surrounded by curious women. He ignored his crowd of apparent admirers, striding on until he came to the palace, where he sat in a throne opposite Hypsipyle. The queen looked away under Jason's direct gaze, but she was first to speak. She told Jason a story of how the Lemnian men had turned against their wives, preferring captive women instead, until finally the Lemnian women refused to allow the men to come ashore after yet another raid on the Thracians. The men, she continued, asked for all the male children then left to live in Thrace. Hypsipyle next offered Jason her father's crown if he and his men stayed to father new sons.

Jason returned to the *Argo* to relate Hypsipyle's request to his crew. The Argonauts were only too willing to help, and made their way to the city where the Lemnian women took them to their homes. Heracles and a few others stayed behind, however, and missed out on the dancing and banqueting going on in the town. The legendary warrior grew increasingly frustrated as the weeks passed and the search for the Golden Fleece stalled.

Finally, he felt he had waited long enough, and he gathered the Argonauts together to lecture them and remind them of their duty. The crewmen shuffled their feet in shame under Heracles's admonishing gaze and looked around at each other rather than directly at the great hero. Suitably embarrassed, the Argonauts prepared to go back to their ship. The Lemnian women begged them to return, but even the queen herself could not stop the Argonauts leaving. She turned to Jason and pleaded for him to come back when he had finished his quest, so that she could be a proper mother to any child she might have as a result of their brief affair. Jason replied that if he did not return she was to send the child to Iolcus.

With that, Jason embarked followed by his Argonauts. Argus cast off the ropes, and the men pulled on their oars, leaving Lemnos in their wake. If any of the Argonauts thought they had left their troubles behind, though, they were about to receive a terrible shock.

The Monstrous Sacrifice

With Lemnos receding into the distance behind them, the Argonauts prepared for their voyage through the Hellespont. Good breezes brought the *Argo* quickly to the coast of Segeum, where the Argonauts drew in for the night. Heracles and Telamon set out to walk along the shore while the crew pitched their tents and lit fires for their meals. They had not gone far when

Statue of Jason holding the Golden Fleece. (Fabrizio Troiani/Alamy)

they heard the lament of a young woman, pleading for her life. The two Argonauts ran down the shore to a small village, where Heracles spotted a shackled woman on a crag. He shouted up to her, asking why she was in this predicament. She replied that she had been drawn by lot as a sacrifice to a sea monster that terrorized the area. She begged Heracles for help, but even as she did so a terrible roar rang out, and the monster emerged from the sea.

The serpentine creature's coils flowed along behind the upraised neck upon which its fearsome head jutted forward, displaying three rows of razor sharp fangs. On the monster came, driven by a howling wind and raging sea toward its sacrificial meal. Telamon glanced sideways at Heracles, who was already incanting a prayer to the gods and preparing his weapons. Heracles leaped on to a rock between the monster and its target and fired his bow, sending arrow after arrow into the raised neck of the beast. Still the monster plowed on, ignoring the pinpricks on its thick hide. Heracles jumped into the water in a fury, smashing the monster with a rock, then following up with his war club to deliver the final crushing blows.

Telamon ran to fetch the rest of the Argonauts, who stared in amazement at the sea turned red with the monster's blood. Heracles, meanwhile, climbed up to free the young sacrifice that would no longer be needed. Below, the local inhabitants rejoiced, but the Argonauts did not linger for long as they had to be on their way.

The Mount of Bears

Liberated from Lemnos and still eager from Heracles's killing of the monster, the Argonauts put their backs into rowing across the empty sea. At sunset, a south wind caught the sail, providing the men with relief and pushing the little ship into the Hellespont. On they sailed, through day and night, tacking their way up the narrow body of water until they broke through into the wider Propontis, the modern day Sea of Marmara. Their next stop would be an island known to locals as the Mount of Bears.

The sight that greeted Jason's crew as they sailed toward the island was one of fields blanketing the slopes of a prominent mountain and flowing down to a very shallow isthmus. It was a peaceful scene but one that disguised the dangers ahead, because the inhabitants of the island, the Doliones, faced a fearsome enemy that lived on the high ground. They were the Gegenees, a fierce tribe of six-armed giants. The Doliones and their king, Cyzicus, lived on the plain around the isthmus under the protection of Poseidon, who kept the Gegenees at bay. When they saw the *Argo*'s square sail rising over the horizon, the Doliones rushed down to the shore to greet the strangers.

Cyzicus was still a young man, newly married, and that placed upon him the duty of protecting his people. But he had heard a prophecy that a band of heroes would arrive, and that when they did, he was to meet them with

Heracles (better known in the modern world as Hercules) took a break from his labors to join the crew of the *Argo*.

friendship, not war. The king therefore ordered a banquet for his guests, and mingled with them, asking who they were and from where they had sailed. He found out quickly about the quest for the Golden Fleece, and he told the Argonauts in return about the peoples and places in the vicinity, but he did not know any more than local knowledge. The feast continued well into the night, but Jason was determined to climb the mountain in the morning and scout the horizons.

When dawn broke, he took some men and trailed up the mountain along a narrow track, not knowing that they were under hostile surveillance. Once at the top, their first action was to order that the ship be brought around to anchor in the harbor at Chytus, on the other side of the island. The watching Gegenees seized this opportune moment, however, to launch their attack on the ship.

The Gegenees raced down the mountainside to intercept the *Argo* from the rocks around the harbor entrance. They hurled rocks down from their vantage point, but they had reckoned without Heracles, who had remained behind with some crewmen to guard the ship and steer it into safe harbor. He picked up his massive war bow and unleashed a storm of arrows, each one finding a target

The *Argo* painted by Konstantinos Volanakis.

Bronze Age Ships and Seafaring

Not all Bronze Age ships received the direct blessings of a goddess as Jason's *Argo* did, but in all other aspects his ship was typical for the age. The Mycenaean Greeks were the pre-eminent seafarers during the time that Jason's voyage probably took place. Their warships, in particular, were suited for close-to-shore navigation and raiding into estuaries—where rivers open up into seas—and up rivers. The *Argo* was such a vessel, at about ninety feet long and ten feet wide, with room for twenty-five rowers on each side, each occupying only three feet of space.

The only open deck areas were at the front and rear of the ship, connected by a walkway down the center; therefore, the crew had to stow their equipment under their benches. Both the front and rear of the vessel were curved, though a horizontal beam projected from the front at sea level; this was to aid stability and make it easier to beach the ship when required.

There was a single mast hoisted by ropes into the vertical position and secured by a mast box toward the middle of the ship, and a basic rudder system at the rear to help steer, made up of a tiller and steering oar. The single large sail was sewn from linen patches and operated by leather or papyrus ropes running from the front of the ship to the rear. The navigator pulled on the ropes to set the sail into the wind as desired. The ship also weighed very little, and was designed with a shallow draft. That made it difficult to navigate over rough seas, but ideal for the river work so often found in the story of Jason and his Argonauts.

among the Gegenees. Meanwhile, Jason and his force of Argonauts sprinted down the mountain, unleashing a barrage of arrows and spears into the now-trapped Gegenees until all of them fell dead. Once the fighting was over, Jason ordered the Gegenees' corpses be laid in rows along the beach, with their bodies half in the water so that both the fish and birds could feed on them.

After a brief rest, the reunited crew of the *Argo* decided to head out to sea, hoping to get back on track with their quest.

The *Argo* sailed away, all day and into the night. Unfortunately, the wind turned the ship around in the dark, so that when the tired Argonauts threw their hawsers onto the rocks and stepped ashore, they were unaware they had returned to the land of the Doliones. They weren't alone in their error, as the Doliones didn't recognize the returning Argonauts, believing them instead to be a Macrian war party. The Doliones hastily donned their armor and armed themselves before rushing down to repel the intruders.

The ensuing fight was fierce but short: the Doliones found themselves hopelessly outmatched by the Argonauts. Heracles killed two, as did Peleus; Acastus and Telamon took down one warrior each. More Doliones fell, but their greatest loss was their king, killed when Jason drove a spear through his breastplate. The rest fled back to the city as fast as they could run.

It was only when the sun came up that both sides realized their grievous error. The Argonauts were particularly shocked to discover the body of Cyzicus lying in front of them. For the next three days, they lamented along with the remaining Doliones. The king's body was buried with full funeral rites, his tragic death compounded by his new bride committing suicide in her grief.

Violent storms raged over the island for the next twelve days, preventing the *Argo* from sailing. On the twelfth night, while the Argonauts slept under the watchful guard of Acastus and Mopsus the seer, a bird hovered over Jason's head. Mopsus heard the bird's claim that the storm would soon abate, and immediately woke his captain. He told Jason that he must climb to the temple on Mount Dindymum and ask for help from Rhea, the mother of the gods.

The news energized Jason, who quickly woke the rest of the crew and told them of the prophecy. Some of the men gathered two oxen, and, after rowing the ship round to the next harbor, the Argonauts set off up the mountain. When they reached the summit, the crew set up an altar of stones and raised a fire for the sacrifice. While Jason offered libations, the others danced around in their armor, banging their swords on their shields. This pleased Rhea greatly, and she gave the Argonauts a sign by growing flowers around their feet and bringing out the woodland animals. The goddess also caused a spring to gush, forever after known as the Spring of Jason.

Satisfied, the Argonauts trekked back down the hill to the *Argo*. The storms abated overnight, and the grateful heroes finally left the Island of Bears.

The Loss of Heracles

Despite not being the leader of the expedition, the great warrior Heracles had been the most influential crewmember. It was Heracles who stood guard whenever the ship was brought to anchor, and he had acted as the moral guide in Lemnos, reminding the Argonauts of their mission to bring back the Golden Fleece. At sea, when the wind dropped, Heracles powered the *Argo* from his rowing position in the middle of the ship. Not surprisingly, therefore, it was mainly through Heracles's strength that the *Argo* raced away from the Island of Bears, towards the Mysian mainland. Then, suddenly, to the legend's amazement, his oar broke in the increasingly rough sea.

Like most ships of the time, the *Argo* stayed within sight of land whenever possible. (Mary Evans Picture Library / Alamy)

This forced Jason to pull in near the outfall of the River Cius, but thankfully on land belonging to the friendly Mysians. The natives brought food and supplies down to the ship, and the Argonauts got on with preparing an appropriate feast for the occasion. The single-minded Heracles, however, only had thoughts for getting wood to make a new oar.

While the others prepared the feast, Heracles walked off into the woods, looking for a suitable tree without too many leaves or branches. He soon located a useful candidate for his oar, laid down his bow and quiver, and took off his lion-skin cloak. He swung his bronze-tipped club at the base of the tree to loosen it; then, anchoring himself to the ground in a wide stance, Heracles pulled the trunk from the ground. Pleased with his work, he gathered his equipment and cloak, and, with the tree balanced on his shoulder, began his trek back to the ship.

Heracles's youthful assistant Hylas had watched his hero walk off into the forest, and then busied himself getting ready for Heracles's return. He picked up his bronze pitcher and made his way to a spring that lay not too far inside the tree line. As Hylas knelt down to fill the pitcher, he did not see the water nymph rising nearby. Hylas's youth and beauty struck the water nymph with such force that she could not resist. She had to have him, and she reached up for a kiss, placing one arm round the startled young man's neck while the other drew him down into the water.

Back at the camp, Polyphemus was also waiting for Heracles when he heard Hylas cry out. Polyphemus drew his sword and ran into the woods, believing wild animals or robbers had attacked the youth. Rather than finding Hylas, however, Polyphemus ran into Heracles, whom he quickly told of his fear for Hylas. The legendary hero dropped the tree in sudden rage and sprinted along the path in the direction from which the startled cry had come, but the boy was nowhere to be seen. Heracles searched through the night, his shouts echoing through the trees, but none of the other Argonauts heard his cries, or knew what was going on down the beach from where they spent the night resting from their feast.

When dawn came, Tiphys urged the crew on board to catch the wind. The excited Argonauts drew up the anchors, cast off the lines, and hoisted the sail, which the wind filled to carry the *Argo* out to sea. Only then, with the Poseidian headland well behind them, did they notice the absence of Heracles, Hylas, and Polyphemus. Jason sat in shocked silence and horror at the loss of their talismanic hero. Telamon, however, thought he saw another motive in his captain, and turned on him, accusing Jason of deliberately leaving Heracles behind so that the legend could not steal all the glory if the mission proved successful. He jumped up and dashed towards Tiphys to make him turn the ship around and fetch Heracles.

Zetes and Calaïs tried to stop Telamon but, as they did, Glaucus, a god renowned for his prophetic abilities, rose from the sea and grabbed the ship's keel. He pointed out to the frightened Argonauts that to go back for the missing men was to interfere with Zeus's wishes: Heracles's destiny was to complete his twelve labors, while Polyphemus would found a great city. Glaucus then plunged back into the sea, rocking the little boat and its shaken crew. Glaucus's words had their desired effect on Telamon, and he immediately apologized to Jason, who equally quickly forgave the hotheaded Argonaut.

With calm restored on board, the *Argo* once more caught the wind and sailed on through the night, drawing Jason ever nearer to his encounter with the Golden Fleece.

Book II: The Voyage to Colchis

The Bebrycian Boxing Match

The Argonauts sailed until they beached for the night on land belonging to Amycus, the arrogant king of the Bebrycians. Amycus believed that no one could beat him at boxing, and had decreed that anyone attempting to leave his lands must fight him first. The king's many victories over his neighbors led him to believe that these newcomers would prove equally weak, and he set off down to the beach to confront the Argonauts. Jason's crew grew steadily angrier as they listened to Amycus's challenge. Polydeuces in particular became angered, and he stepped forward to champion the Argonauts. Amycus glared like a cornered lion while Polydeuces took off his fine cloak, a present from a Lemnian woman. The king's cloak was of much rougher cloth, like the man himself, and he threw it down in contempt.

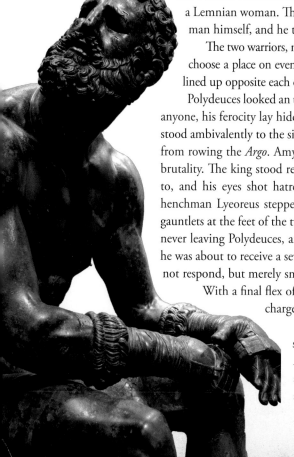

The statue of the Thermae Boxer from the third–second century BCE provides a good example of the boxing gloves worn by the Ancient Greeks.

The two warriors, now both fully committed to the fight, drew apart to choose a place on even ground. The rest of the Argonauts and Bebrycians lined up opposite each other, behind their respective champions.

Polydeuces looked an unlikely champion; although large enough to fight anyone, his ferocity lay hidden behind his youth and seeming innocence. He stood ambivalently to the side, flexing hands that were knotted and hardened from rowing the *Argo*. Amycus, on the other hand, could barely contain his brutality. The king stood ready to tear this upstart limb from limb if he had to, and his eyes shot hatred toward the young Argonaut. Then Amycus's henchman Lyoreus stepped forward and placed two pairs of dry, rawhide gauntlets at the feet of the two fighters. Amycus picked his gloves up, his eyes never leaving Polydeuces, and he taunted the younger man, telling him that he was about to receive a severe lesson from a mighty warrior. Polydeuces did not respond, but merely smiled while Castor and Talaus fitted his gauntlets. With a final flex of his fists, Polydeuces stepped back to wait for the charge he knew was coming from the bullish king.

Amycus crashed into Polydeuces like a stormy sea hitting the shore, his fists pummelling the Argonaut, blow after blow landing in unending attack. Polydeuces parried and pushed back against the onslaught, his punches slicing through

BRONZE AGE WARFARE

Placing the voyage of the Argonauts in its correct historical context affects the range and nature of the weapons and armor available to Jason's warriors. Moreover, later interpolations into the legend may have introduced anachronistic methods of fighting not appropriate to Jason's era. As a result, we cannot know for certain what the Argonauts wore in combat, but we can make an educated guess.

The common weapons of the late Bronze Age were the spear, sword, dagger, and bow. Spears were probably the most common but lacked uniformity. Earlier spears held leaf-shaped blades up to 20 in long, but later spearheads were half that size and much narrower, suggesting they were lighter, and some might have been thrown in the style of javelins. Warriors may also have carried a pairing of a heavy spear and a lighter one. Swords too became shorter, from 35 in to 15 in, on average. Daggers, on the other hand, became longer, obscuring the differences between the two bladed weapons. We are told that one Argonaut sailed with a huge double-edged axe, perhaps emphasizing his legendary status, but these were not common weapons. The use of bows developed from hunting, and therefore most warriors would be familiar with their use, and they would have been the primary ranged weapon.

Plate armor in the form of cuirass, a piece of armor that covered the body from the neck to the waist; bracers, which covered the arms or the wrists; and greaves to cover the shins was in use in Bronze Age warfare, but a small raiding party such as the Argonauts would have decried its use. They probably would have preferred more lightweight personal protection such as bronze greaves for their lower legs, a thick padded linen cuirass most likely accompanied by a single bronze shoulderpiece, and bronze or leather forearm protectors. Head protection was afforded by leather helmets covered in boar ivory or small bronze discs; the full bronze helmets associated with later Greek hoplites were not yet developed.

Finally, the Argonauts carried shields, though exactly what kind is difficult to determine. Two types of shield were common in the Greek Bronze Age. Tower shields were large, hide-covered, and wooden-framed, with flat bottoms and arched tops. The other shield was the figure-of-eight shield that was similarly wooden-framed and hide-covered. Either shield would have offered significant protection, and both were particularly useful for crouching behind with spear or sword at the ready.

the king's rushing fists. Both men stood their ground, exchanging hit for hit, blow for blow. Heads butting, teeth rattling, punch after punch landed in search of the kill. The men and women on both sides cheered as their champions drew apart for a moment, but just a moment, before they lunged forward again to resume their death match. The battering continued, the weary fighters exchanging furious punches, pain and desperation etched on their faces.

(Overleaf) The Boxing Match of Polydeuces and Amycus. Boxing is a reoccurring theme in the myths and legends of Ancient Greece. Most famously, it appears in the *Iliad* as one of the games held to honor Patroclus after his death. It is in his honor that boxing is later added to the Olympic Games.

Then, sensing his time had come, Amycus closed in for the kill. He stretched up on his toes to bring his fist down on the impertinent youth's head in a fatal hammer blow. At the last second, Polydeuces swerved, taking the king's strike on his shoulder while landing his own lightning counterpunch just above Amycus's ear. The bones inside the king's ear shattered, and he dropped to his knees. Swaying there, he then rolled on to the ground, his life already departed.

The Bebrycians stood mute, in shock, staring at their dead king for a moment, before picking up their spears and clubs and rushing at the unarmed Polydeuces. They were quick, but the Argonauts were quicker, drawing their swords and taking up positions in front of their champion. Castor struck first, cleaving an attacker's head in two. Polydeuces still had enough fight in him to drop-kick one man and then punch another so hard he tore off the man's brow above his eye. The Bebrycians drew blood too, but the battle ended when Ancaeus raised his massive war-axe and plunged into the barbarians, followed by Jason and two other furious Argonauts.

The leaderless tribesmen cowered under this sudden onslaught, then broke and fled. The Argonauts followed up their victory by plundering all around. One commented that if they had not abandoned Heracles there would have been no challenge from Amycus; others argued, however, that this latest test was the will of Zeus. The Argonauts returned to the beach to make their offerings to the gods and tend their wounded.

They set sail the next morning into the treacherous Bosporus, relying on Tiphys's navigational skills to steer the *Argo* towards a safe harbor opposite Bithynia. Here they would encounter a tortured old man, and learn their destiny.

Polydeuces and Amycus by
José Daniel Cabrera Peña.

Phineas and the Harpies

By any standards, Phineas had lived a strenuous existence. He had been given the gift of prophecy as a young man but, through divining the future indiscriminately, he had usurped a critical power of Zeus. Divine retribution came in the form of blindness and perpetual old age, to which Zeus added still more torment by means of the vile flying creatures known to all as the Harpies.

Whenever local people asked Phineas to divine the will of the gods, and left offerings in payment, the Harpies descended from the skies, tearing away the old man's food with their hooked beaks and leaving behind such a stench that any remaining scraps became so foully tainted that no one would come near Phineas to help him eat.

By the time the Argonauts approached his home, Phineas survived in a wretched state; his body, caked in filth, trembled with age, starvation and weariness, held together only by the strength of his gift. Hope burst within Phineas, however, upon hearing the trampling feet of his latest visitors, because Zeus had also declared that a band of warriors would help him finally taste his food. Phineas shuffled to the door, sat down, and waited.

The old prophet's physical condition shocked the Argonauts when they reached his home. Phineas took no notice of their concerns, and spoke resolutely. He knew who they were, and of their dangerous mission, but he begged them to first help alleviate his misery at the hands of the Harpies. Phineas added that an oracle had foretold that the sons of Boreas—Zetes and Calaïs—would do the deed. The old man's appeal reduced the adventurers to tears, and they all wanted to help him, but they were still wary of offending the gods.

In 1984, British writer and explorer Tim Severin retraced the voyage of Jason from Iolcus to Colchis in a specially built replica of the *Argo*. The next year, he released his book *The Jason Voyage*, recounting the journey. (Topfoto)

Zetes stepped forward and, taking Phineas's hand, asked for reassurance that it was safe to give their assistance. The prophet replied that he would take responsibility for their actions and that the gods would not harm them. The brothers, comforted by the prophet's guarantee, drew back to plan the demise of the Harpies.

Zetes and Calaïs prepared an ambush for the Harpies by setting out a feast for Phineas in the customary fashion. When Phineas ambled up to the food, the warriors drew their swords and hid nearby. Barely had Phineas touched his first bite when the Harpies plunged through the clouds, with their talons and beaks extended to grab the food. The Argonauts leaped out of hiding, but the Harpies were too quick and grabbed all the food, leaving behind their distinctive stench.

Determined to end the Harpies's reign of terror on the old prophet, the winged brothers took off in pursuit. Hunters and hunted swooped through the sky, Zetes and Calaïs closing with every wing-beat until they came within inches of latching on to the terrified Harpies. Then, all of a sudden, the goddess Iris appeared. She told the two men that to kill the Harpies would indeed go against the will of Zeus, but she pledged that if the brothers spared them, she would see that they never came near Phineas again. Zetes and Calaïs, their mission accomplished, turned back to tell their comrades the good news.

While they waited for the brothers to return, the rest of the Argonauts tended to Phineas by bathing him and preparing one of Amycus's sheep for a suitable victory feast. The prophet, freed from his curse, ate ravenously alongside Jason's crew before joining them in their vigil for the returning Zetes and Calaïs. Suitably fed and rested by the fire, and surrounded by the

Zetes chasing after a harpy by José Daniel Cabrera Peña.

(Overleaf) The Harpies. Ancient sources usually described the Harpies as beautiful women with wings. It is not until the Middle-Ages that the Harpies were re-imagined as the hideous bird-women that are more common in modern depictions. This artwork depicts them in the more modern style, which seems more appropriate to their role of tormentors and despoilers in the story of Jason.

Argonauts, Phineas began to speak. He first warned the men that he had learned his lesson about the use of prophecy, which only Zeus could impart in full. Therefore, what he had to tell them about their continuing journey must, by necessity, be incomplete. That said, he continued, they would soon come to the Symplegades, rocks at the junction of two seas.

These rocks were not anchored but clashed against each other, crushing anything caught between them. If the Argonauts tried to rush through blindly, moreover, they would surely die. Rather, they must send a dove through first, and if it made it, then the Argonauts must use all their strength on the oars to pull themselves through after the bird. Of course, if the bird got crushed, they would have to turn back and try again.

Phineas proceeded to tell the Argonauts what would come after they navigated safely through the rocks. Much of it was a description of places and tribes they would encounter, and some that they should avoid, until they came to the end of their journey at the shady grove of Ares, where a massive and ever-vigilant serpent lay curled round the oak tree that held the Golden Fleece. The old man's declaration stunned the Argonauts into silence as the dangers ahead sunk in to their imaginations. Jason was clearly dismayed, and asked Phineas how they would ever get back to Greece even if they managed to secure the Fleece. The prophet told him not to worry about that, because a goddess would show them the way, though they would return by a different route. Before he could say more, however, Zetes and Calaïs flew in to tell the men of their success against the Harpies.

The Harpies by José Daniel Cabrera Peña.

The Argonauts celebrated their victory before Jason turned again to Phineas. He said that it was obvious that at least one god cared for Phineas, and that maybe that meant the old man could regain his sight. But Phineas waved him off, proclaiming that his eyes were useless, and, besides, what he wished for most was a swift death to relieve his suffering.

Jason and Phineas made small talk for a while in the pre-dawn light, and, when the sun rose, the local Thynian people came to hear the old man's oracles. Phineas patiently dealt with each request throughout the rest of the day. When his friend Paraebius arrived, Phineas asked him to fetch two sheep fit for an evening feast. When it was time to prepare the fire for the sheep, Phineas called on Jason, Zetes, and Calaïs to perform the devotion to Apollo, the god of prophecy. Their prayers complete, the crew settled down to their feast before turning in for the night.

They hoped to sail the next morning, but, while they slept, the Etesian winds began to blow, stranding the *Argo*. For days afterwards, Jason's crew had little to do but watch the daily procession of Thynians seeking Phineas's counsel. The winds eventually dropped, and the Argonauts were finally able to row out to sea, not forgetting to bring with them a white dove.

The Clashing Rocks

It did not take long for the *Argo* to reach the dreaded clashing rocks. A winding strait surrounded by cliffs marked the entrance to the channel where the rocks promised a violent welcome for unsuspecting travellers, but what truly heralded their location was the awful din created by the rocks constantly crashing together and then falling back. Euphemus grabbed the dove in anticipation, so that when they rounded the last bend he was ready to let the bird fly. The terrified Argonauts watched Euphemus release the dove,

The *Argo* heads for the Clashing Rocks. (*Look and Learn*)

then their gaze followed the desperate bird as it flew into the widening chasm created as the rocks drew apart. Sensing movement, the rocks sprang forward again, casting a massive cloud of spray over the *Argo*.

Jason's crew could only hear the roar of the surf surging in and out of the caves under the cliffs, and feel the current whip the *Argo* round. Amidst the disorientating violence of noise and movement, however, they could see clearly that although the rocks had stripped the dove's tail feathers, the bird had made it through. The rocks drew apart once more: now was the time to strike. Tiphys called on the Argonauts to pull on their oars with everything they had.

Jason (Jason London) guides the *Argo* through the Clashing Rocks in this still from the 2000 made-for-television movie. (AF archive / Alamy)

The rowers took up Tiphys's challenge and pulled, knowing their lives depended on it. Their anxiety turned into terror, however, when the tide proved too strong to overcome and began to drag the *Argo* back into the killing zone. When a huge wave rose up before them, the crew instinctively ducked, believing their end had come, but Tiphys masterfully eased the battered ship over the crest, and the Argonauts sighed with relief as the wave rolled away behind them. Then Euphemus stood and urged the rowers to put in more effort. The Argonauts redoubled their efforts, bending the oars almost to their breaking point, desperately trying to force their way past the closing rocks. Another wave struck the ship, holding it in the maelstrom amid a tempest of noise and violence. Just when all seemed lost, however, Athena rose up out of the water and held the rocks back with her left hand while, with her right, she pushed the *Argo* forward over the deadly waves.

The ship only just made it into the calm waters beyond the clashing rocks, the exhausted crew slumping over their oars. Athena returned to Olympus, her work done, leaving behind the rocks fused together forever, as foretold in an oracle. No sailor would ever again have to go through the ordeal of the Argonauts.

One man remained unhappy: Jason. After the ship had sailed into safer waters, Tiphys turned to his captain to remind him that Phineas's prophecies were coming true and that, with the divine aid of Athena, this quest would now go much more smoothly. Jason thought for a moment before baring his

Euphemus releases the dove to fly between the Clashing Rocks.
(*Look and Learn*)

soul to Tiphys and the rest of the crew. He told them how he had made a mistake in accepting this mission, and that he was afraid, not only for himself but for every soul on board the ship. The Argonauts shouted encouragement in return, lifting Jason out of his despair until he asked for calm.

This time he told them that their courage had set an example for him, and that from this moment he would no longer live in fear of what lay ahead. With harmony restored and the dreadful clashing rocks behind them, the Argonauts again took up their oars and pulled. On through the day and night they rowed until they came to the deserted island of Thynias.

Apollo and Lycus

It was a very weary crew indeed that pulled the *Argo* onto the beach at Thynias. Just as they did, however, a remarkable event occurred that gave them energy once more. Who saw him first was never made clear, but the Argonauts were completely taken aback by the sudden appearance of Apollo flying through the skies above them. The god was unmistakeable, with his long golden hair and silver bow, and, as he passed, the ground rumbled and quaked, and the surf surged up the beach. Jason's crew bowed their heads, fearing to stare into the god's eyes, and remained that way until Apollo disappeared over the horizon.

Orpheus broke their awestruck silence, telling his comrades that they must call this island the Isle of Apollo and make a suitable offering in his honor. The Argonauts immediately made an altar from the shingle, found a goat for the sacrifice, and sang and danced in celebration. When a fresh west wind blew up on their third morning on the Isle of Apollo, the crew prepared their ship and sailed away.

The *Argo* sped along all that day and on into the night, when, abruptly, the wind failed, compelling the Argonauts to take up their oars once more. By dawn, though, they came in sight of the Acherusian headland, and the relieved sailors pulled up in its shelter. Watching the ship sail in was the local king, Lycus, along with an excited crowd of people. The news of the Argonauts' defeat of the hated Bebrycians had spread like wildfire, and Lycus ordered a feast prepared for the arriving heroes. He singled out Polydeuces for particular attention, but all of the Argonauts were mobbed and taken into the city to celebrate.

For their part, the Argonauts told of their adventures so far, the trials passed, and the sacrifices given in pursuit of the fabled Golden Fleece. Lycus listened intently before addressing Jason and his crew. The king began by grieving for the loss of Heracles, and acknowledging his debt to the Argonauts as a neighbor of the Bebrycians. To that end, he offered to build a temple that all could see, and he ordered his son Dascylus to join the crew and guide them to Colchis. The banquet lasted all night. At dawn, the Argonauts once more started to board their ship, full of hope and confidence as they prepared to set sail, but tragedy lurked nearby.

(Opposite) The Clashing Rocks. The Argonauts release a dove to fly between the Clashing Rocks, as suggested by Phineas. The Argonauts have the ship's mast in place in order to check the wind, before they make their run between the rocks.

Disaster Strikes

Idmon the soothsayer was as keen as anyone to get back on board the *Argo*. However as he rushed along the riverbank towards the ship, he did not see a huge white boar cooling itself in the mud. The boar, however, saw Idmon. The enraged animal rushed out of the reeds and crashed into the startled young prophet. One of its dagger-like tusks tore through bone and muscle, dropping Idmon to the muddy ground. The Argonauts ran to the sound of Idmon's screams and came upon the dreadful scene. Peleus drove the boar back with his spear, but the animal turned and charged again, only for Idas to impale it on his spear. The rest of the crew picked up Idmon and carried him back to the *Argo*, where he died in their arms. The Argonauts and King Lycus grieved for three days, then buried Idmon in a specially raised barrow.

Calamity struck again almost immediately, when Tiphys suddenly fell ill and died. The Argonauts buried their navigator beside the young seer, and made their way down to the shore, where they sat in desolate silence at this latest cruel turn of events. Most of the crew thought their quest was now at an end, and they rapidly lost hope at ever returning to Greece. The goddess Hera took note of the crew's despair, however, and breathed courage into Ancaeus. He stood and addressed his comrades, pointing out that he came on this voyage not as a warrior but as a seaman, and, besides, any of them could pilot the ship with the required skill.

The *Argo* by José Daniel Cabrera Peña.

Peleus stood up too to exhort the Argonauts, but Jason was less easily moved. He asked which of them was a skilled steersman, because he could not see one, and he feared they were stuck facing a wretched fate. Ancaeus would not listen to Jason's pessimism, and offered to take on the steering duties himself, to which the rest of the Argonauts, including Jason, agreed. They all rallied round and prepared to sail.

The Birds of Ares

It was dawn on the twelfth day before the Argonauts finally left Lycus's kingdom. They took up their oars until clear of the river mouth, then shook out the sail, which caught the wind and spread. The *Argo* bucked and plowed through the waves. As they passed the headland that contained the grave of Sthenelus—a former comrade of Heracles—they saw his ghost wearing a gleaming four-peaked helmet with a blood-red crest. The Argonauts sat in awe at the sight until Mopsus insisted that they land and honor Sthenelus. Jason ordered the ship to shore, where they quickly tied her up and set off for the gravesite. Once there, they offered libations and sacrificed sheep. Orpheus dedicated his lyre, giving his name to the headland, Lyra.

The wind blew strong again when the *Argo* resumed its voyage, carrying it across the sea like a bird in flight. They passed the stream of Parthenius, then Sesamus, Erythini, Crobialus, Cromna, and Cytorus. The *Argo* sailed on day and night along the Assyrian coast towards the land of the Amazons, a fearsome tribe of women warriors. Finally, when the seas became too rough and dangerous, Jason ordered the *Argo* into shore for shelter, even though the local tribes might prove hostile. The breeze soon rose again, however, and they set sail quickly to avoid any potential fight.

After another day of favorable winds, the *Argo* reached Chaldia, where the inhabitants, the Chalybes, eschewed farming for working the iron deposits that littered the land. The little ship then rounded the next headland, sailing past the land of the Tibareni, whose men took to their beds when their women gave birth. The Mossynoeci, who lived further along the coast, were even more bizarre; whatever was private in everyone else's culture was public in their world, and vice-versa, so that even intimate family life was a public spectacle. Jason and the Argonauts were therefore happy to sail past the Mossynoeci too.

The Argonauts made good time until they reached the island of Ares. Here the breeze dropped just as night began to fall, stranding the *Argo* out to sea. The sailors reached for their oars, paying little attention to a single bird flying above them, though some watched as it shook its wings until a feather fell out. The feather dropped like a lead weight and pierced Oileus's shoulder, causing him to drop his oar. Eribotes pulled out the feather and tended to the wound, but just then another bird appeared and dived towards the ship. Clytius brought down this new attacker with an arrow of his own.

Amphidamas shouted a warning that arrows would not help if a flock of such birds attacked, and that they needed a better plan if they were to get safely to the beach. He told the crew that even Heracles could not fight birds with arrows; rather, he used a bronze rattle to frighten them away. Amphidamas suggested something similar for the Argonauts. He told them to put on their war helmets and protect the ship with shields and spears, then row until the birds came. When they did, the Argonauts were to shout as loud as they could and bang on their shields. The sight and sound of the Argonauts, added Amphidamas, would scare the birds away.

The Argonauts followed Amphidamas's advice to the letter. They quickly donned their gleaming bronze helmets, the blood-red crests shaking in the breeze. Half of the crew began to row towards the beach while the rest locked their shields to form a roof over the *Argo*. When all was set, they began shouting at the top of their lungs. They saw no birds yet, but as the ship reached shore, the warriors banged on their shields and a dark cloud of birds rose, showering the *Argo* with feathers before retreating over the nearby mountains. The Argonauts, having avoided any further casualties, settled down on the beach for the night, but the arrival of morning held a further surprise.

Shipwreck of the sons of Phrixus. *(Look and Learn)*

The Sons of Phrixus

Far away from the island of Ares and the drama unfolding over the Argonauts, the four sons of Phrixus had earlier boarded a Colchian ship bound for Greece. That night, a storm struck from the north when they were passing the island, wrecking their ship and throwing the brothers into the sea. They clung to a beam until, drenched and shaking all over, they washed up on the island. The storm had died down by first light and soon the brothers found themselves walking towards a band of fearsome warriors coming down the beach to investigate.

The shipwrecked brothers pleaded with the strangers to provide some clothes and supplies. At that, Jason stepped forward from the group to offer them help, but he was curious as to how the men came to be there. One, Argos, introduced himself and his brothers—Cytissorus, Phrontis, and Melas—as the sons of Phrixus, who had fled with the fabled Golden Fleece to Colchis. Jason replied excitedly that the brothers were kin to him on his father's side, and welcomed them as friends. The other Argonauts could hardly believe their ears at this news, and rushed to get clothes and food for the men. The crew and the brothers then built an altar of pebbles to Ares, and sacrificed a sheep in his honor.

During their celebration feast, an ebullient Jason turned to the brothers, offering them a place on his crew. He also told them where he was heading, and asked them to act as guides. Far from the gratitude Jason expected, however, the brothers looked at him in horror. Surely, they asked, Jason did not expect the king of Colchis, Aeëtes, to willingly hand over the Golden Fleece? Argos pointed out to the Argonauts that they may be great warriors but Aeëtes ruled with an iron fist, and had many soldiers at his disposal. Moreover, the Fleece lay under the protection of a massive and ever-vigilant serpent.

The Argonauts visibly paled at the image Argos conjured of the trials that awaited them, but Peleus answered that the Argonauts were a match for anyone, and doubted that the Colchian tribes would interfere in their righteous quest. The Argonauts now nodded their heads in agreement with Peleus. The matter settled, and having finished their meal, they turned in for the night. A breeze greeted the dawn, and Jason's crew, along with the brothers, boarded the *Argo* and sailed away from the island of Ares, their destination: Colchis.

Colchis

The *Argo* sailed on, aided by a stiff wind, past the island of Philyra and the lands of the Becheiri, Sapeires, and Byzeres. The Argonauts saw the Caucasus Mountains, and the enormous eagle that was assigned by the gods to repeatedly eat Prometheus's liver as punishment for his stealing the gift of fire. Not long after the eagle soared out of view, the disturbed sailors heard Prometheus's screams echo across the waves.

That night, the *Argo*, under the expert guidance of Argos, sailed into the estuary of the River Phasis. The Argonauts quickly stowed the sail and mast, and rowed into the fast-flowing mouth of the wide river. On their left they could see the mountains and the Colchian city of Aea, while, on their right, the Plain of Ares stretched away towards the sacred grove in which dwelt the serpent guarding the Fleece.

Jason poured out libations of honey and wine to the gods and the souls of dead heroes, asking them to look favorably on his intrusion into their domain. But it was Ancaeus who spoke to remind the crew that this was the time to decide on the best strategy for securing the Fleece. Argos therefore directed the *Argo* into a shady backwater where they could rest before undertaking the most vital and dangerous part of their mission.

Book III: The Golden Fleece

Medea

All the bravado displayed by Jason's warriors while settling down in the shadow of Colchis did not fool Hera and Athena. They knew that Aeëtes ruled his kingdom despotically, and that neither taking the Fleece by force, nor persuasion, guaranteed Jason ultimate success. The goddesses therefore drew apart from the rest of the gods, so that they too could ponder and discuss possible winning strategies. After a while, Hera looked up from her thinking and suggested they ask Aphrodite, the goddess of love, to ask her son Eros to make Medea, the daughter of Aeëtes, fall in love with Jason. Athena liked the plan, though she was unsure how it would work. Nevertheless, the two set off with firm resolve to find Aphrodite.

Medea by José Daniel Cabrera Peña.

Aphrodite was still getting ready for the day, when Hera and Athena entered her chambers, and she was none too pleased to see them. She welcomed the goddesses with sarcasm and reproach, because they were not frequent visitors. Hera persevered, however, telling Aphrodite that the final stage of the quest for the Golden Fleece was about to happen, and that she was afraid that Jason might fail without help. Hera added how Jason had earned her patronage through his good deeds, and that she would do whatever she could to honor him and punish King Pelias. Moved by such an appeal, Aphrodite opened her arms to Hera, offering whatever assistance was needed. Hera replied that she wanted Eros to fire his magic arrow into Medea's heart, causing her to fall in love with Jason, and thereby solicit her aid for him in the dangerous tasks he was about to face. Aphrodite was sceptical that her rebellious boy would help, but agreed to ask him. Their mission successful, Hera and Athena left Aphrodite to track down her son.

Eros was in the orchard of Zeus, playing dice with Ganymede, the innocent and beautiful boy whom Zeus had brought to live with the gods. Eros showed Ganymede little respect, however, so that when Aphrodite walked in on them playing, he was taking the last of some golden dice from the hapless child. Ganymede left sullenly, leaving a very happy Eros looking up into the concerned face of his mother. She chided him for his gloating, but promised him a golden ball if he would perform the task she had in mind. The greedy Eros begged for his gift immediately. Aphrodite stood firm, however, and kissed Eros into submission. He therefore willingly picked up his bow and quiver of arrows, and set off down through the heavens to carry out Aphrodite's wishes. Thus the goddesses had done their part to help recover the Golden Fleece, now it would be up to Jason and his crew of heroes to complete the task.

Aeëtes

The Argonauts knew nothing, of course, about the schemes of the gods. As they sat in their ship, hidden among the foliage along the riverbank, they had their own problems to consider. Jason chose this moment, however, to finally stamp his authority on the expedition. He addressed his crew, putting forward the argument that, rather than employing force, he and the sons of Phrixus should go to meet with Aeëtes, and see if he would give up the Fleece through friendship and in recognition of Zeus's will.

The Argonauts agreed unanimously, so Jason and the brothers, along with Telamon and Augeas, set out for Aeëtes's palace. On the way, they passed countless unburied corpses, which served as reminders that the ruthless Colchians neither buried nor cremated their dead. As Hera watched the small group approach, she spread a thick mist through the city, so that they could reach the palace unhindered.

(Opposite) Jason and the Bulls. According to Appollonius, the bulls that Jason used to plow the fields had bronze hooves and snorted fire. Later writers have sometimes taken this one step further and depicted the bulls as either creatures of living bronze or even as fully mechanical constructs.

Jason and his party stared in wonder at the palace complex as they walked through the gates with the fog that had swirled around them now fading. Columns were revealed, orderly lined along the walls, interspersed with vines and foliage in full bloom. Four fountains gushed nearby, one each of oil, milk, wine, and water, and all four crafted by Hephaestus, blacksmith to the gods. Buildings and chambers surrounded the inner court of the palace. Aeëtes and his queen, Eidyia, occupied the tallest building, while his son Apsyrtus lived in a similar tower nearby. Aeëtes's daughters, Chalciope and Medea, also lived in separate towers close to their mother.

Medea's position as priestess of the goddess Hecate meant that she had spent that morning working in the temple. She was out looking for her sister, however, when she first caught sight of the strangers. Her cry of surprise brought Chalciope and her handmaidens running. Chalciope was overjoyed to see her sons and rushed to greet them. Aeëtes and Eidyia and the rest of the household soon arrived to investigate the commotion. None of them, however, saw another unexpected guest flitting through the last tendrils of Hera's mist.

The unseen visitor was Eros on his mission for Aphrodite. He hung back in a doorway where he could clearly see his target. Eros strung his bow, nocked an arrow, and—too rapidly for the human eye to see—darted up to Jason's side before letting his arrow fly and retreating, leaving behind only a soft echo of laughter. Eros's arrow struck Medea in the heart, rendering her speechless and burning with love for Jason. No one around her noticed the arrow's effect on Medea, because they were too busy preparing warm baths and a banquet to celebrate the return of the brothers.

The Golden Fleece by José Daniel Cabrera Peña.

When everyone was rested and refreshed, Aeëtes asked his grandsons why they had returned and who were their companions. The brothers exchanged nervous glances, fearing how Aeëtes would take their news. It was left to Argos, as the eldest brother, to reply to Aeëtes's questions. He told the king how their ship wrecked off the island of Ares, where they met Jason and his Argonauts on the beach. Jason took them in, he continued, providing clothes and food, for which they were grateful, and in return they agreed to accompany Jason to the city. Plunging on with his story, Argos narrated Jason's mission to retrieve the Golden Fleece, and how the gods had helped them to this point. He added that the crew were the sons and grandsons of the immortals.

Aeëtes listened intently, but with increasing anger, as Argos told his story. Then the king could contain his wrath no longer. He ordered the brothers out of his sight and out of Colchis for good. Aeëtes accused them of plotting not to steal the Fleece but his crown, and that if they had not eaten as guests he would have had their tongues hacked out and hands chopped off to prevent them from telling more lies against the gods. A defiant Argos began to reply, but Jason stepped forward and hushed him. He turned to Aeëtes and tried to persuade the king that this mission was genuine.

Jason offered, as compensation, for his crew to fight as mercenaries at the king's will, if he so desired, in return for the Fleece. Aeëtes, having already decided on his course of action, all but ignored Jason's pleading. He said that Jason could have the Fleece, if he proved himself more courageous than the king. To do that, continued Aeëtes, Jason would have to complete two tasks that Aeëtes himself had already performed. The first was to yoke two fire-breathing bulls, and plow the Plain of Ares. If he managed that, Jason was to sow the teeth of a dragon, and, when they grew out of the ground and became armed soldiers, he was to kill them all. If Jason did all that in one day, Aeëtes concluded, he could take the Golden Fleece.

Jason stood in stunned silence at the magnitude of the challenge before him. He had little choice but to accept, of course, to which Aeëtes told him to go and make himself ready for the next day's trials.

Lively Debate

Jason left with Augeias, Telamon, and Argos, leaving the other brothers behind with their mother. Medea watched them leave, filled with passion for Jason, and increasingly distraught over what might happen to him, before she too left to go to her chambers. Argos walked with Jason along the path leading to the ship. He asked Jason not to be offended by what he was about to say, but that he knew of his aunt Medea's skills as a sorceress, and that she could help with the tasks, but he feared she might not. Argos then offered to approach his mother to ask Medea for her assistance.

Far from being insulted, Jason urged Argos to speak to her, even though it

was shameful to accept help from women for what should be a warrior's work. The rest of the Argonauts prevented Argos's immediate reply by surrounding Jason, when he arrived back at the ship. Jason told them of Aeëtes's rage and the tasks that he had agreed to undertake. The crew's clamorous greeting suddenly fell silent as the shock of Jason's words set in.

Peleus broke the silence. He knew that Jason would undertake the tasks, but if he had any doubts then Peleus would willingly replace Jason in the contest. Telamon also stepped in to say he would do it, as did Idas, and Castor and Polydeuces, and finally the youthful Meleager. Argos spoke to the volunteers, pointing out that it was better if they did not throw their lives away needlessly. He added that, with their permission, he would return to the palace and beg his mother to seek the assistance of Medea and her skills as a sorceress.

Suddenly, a dove fell from the sky into Jason's lap, pursued by a hawk that could not pull out of its dive—and which impaled itself on the stern ornament of the *Argo*. Mopsus, who divined prophecies from birds, leapt up to tell the men that this was surely a favorable sign from the gods, and that it was as Phineas foretold about the help a goddess would give them. The Argonauts nodded their approval, all except Idas, who was angered that they should allow mere women to save them.

The crew looked to Jason, but he had already decided that Argos should leave immediately on his mission. He compromised, however, by saying that it was not right for them to hide the *Argo* in a backwater, and that they must move the ship out into the open. Argos left immediately while the Argonauts took up their oars to relocate the *Argo*.

(Opposite) Jason and the Earthborn Men. The origin of the dragon's teeth in the story of Jason and the Argonauts has often been a source of confusion. The teeth sown by Jason do not come from the dragon guarding the Golden Fleece, but instead come from the Dragon of Ares, slain by the hero Cadmus. After Cadmus killed the dragon, he removed its teeth. Half of these he gave to the goddess Athena, who carried them off to Colchis. The other half he sowed into the earth, growing his own crop of earthborn men. These men battled amongst themselves until the survivors joined Cadmus and helped him found the city of Thebes.

Jason plows the field in front of King Aeëtes and the rest of the Argonauts.

The Treacherous King

While Jason and his crew considered their options down by the river, Aeëtes addressed a hastily arranged assembly of Colchians, with treachery in mind. He promised that when the bulls ripped apart whoever was sent to attempt the challenges, he would burn the ship and the crew in it for their arrogance. The Argonauts, he continued, were nothing but pirates, and deserved to be treated as such. The brothers who had brought them here, he thundered, would be sent into exile. To that end, he would keep the ship under surveillance until the moment came to unleash his vengeance.

Argos, meanwhile, approached the palace with some hesitation to speak to Chalciope, who was busy fretting over the possible fate of her four sons at the hands of their vengeful father.

Medea slept fitfully in her chamber, away from the swirl of events surrounding the palace. She dreamed that Jason had come for her, not for the Fleece, and that she would be asked to choose between her father and her future husband. In her dream, she chose the latter, to the anguish of Aeëtes, who cried out, waking Medea from her sleep. Although deeply troubled, she resolved to ask Chalciope to help with the tests.

Medea put on her robe and crept out of her chamber, but she could not bring herself to enter Chalciope's room. Three times she tried, before giving in and returning to throw herself down on her bed, torn between love and duty. A passing handmaiden saw Medea and rushed to Chalciope to tell her of her sister's distress. Her intervention proved timely because the handmaiden found Chalciope sitting with her sons, discussing how to win Medea over to their side in the impending showdown with Aeëtes.

Chalciope rushed over to Medea's room and asked her what was wrong; was she sick or had she heard of some plan by Aeëtes against Chalciope and her sons? Medea could not reveal her feelings for Jason, as that would be a shameful, and potentially fatal, confession. She replied, therefore, that she was worried about what Aeëtes might do to the brothers. Medea waited with bated breath for her sister to speak.

Fear gripped Chalciope and she begged Medea to find some way to help them all, but she insisted that, whether or not she could help, Medea must keep their plans secret. Medea said she wanted to help but did not know how. Chalciope then asked Medea to assist Jason in the contests and revealed that Argos had arrived to appeal for their help. Now that Chalciope had furnished her with a viable excuse to help Jason, Medea pledged herself to her sister's cause, and promised to be at Hecate's temple at dawn with a charm that would work on the bulls.

When Chalciope left, however, Medea's despair over agreeing to help her father's enemy flooded back. Night fell, but still Medea could not sleep for worrying. She possessed the skills and craft to protect Jason from the bulls, but she could not see how to do it without alerting the king, nor how she would greet Jason, if she ever would. Aeëtes would have her executed if he suspected treachery, but that would be no release from her disgrace because her name would forever be synonymous with treason. Medea even contemplated suicide before her infatuation caused her ruin.

She fetched her box of potions, deciding which one would work best to end it all. The watching Hera had seen enough and planted horrifying thoughts of the underworld in Medea's mind, followed by more hopeful images of friends and everything life had to offer. Medea stopped crying at this revelation and put away her box, except for the potions she needed to help Jason. Fortified by her determination to save the man she now loved, Medea could not wait for the sun to rise.

Medea prepared herself to venture out just as the first rays of dawn touched the palace. She dressed in a beautiful robe with a silver veil over her golden hair, while her skin shone with sweet ointment. She carried a potion called the Charm of Prometheus in her belt, made from the sap of a particular flower that grew in the Caucasus, and which, once spread on a man, would protect him from fire. With all in readiness, Medea called for her twelve handmaidens to attend her and make her chariot ready for the journey to the temple. The handmaidens yoked the mules, then Medea mounted the chariot, with two maidens on each side. Medea, reins in one hand and whip in the other, sped along through the town.

When they arrived at the temple, Medea addressed her handmaidens. She told them of her mission that morning and how they would be rewarded if they kept her secret. When Jason arrived at the temple, though, they were to stand back and not interfere. In the meantime, they would sing to keep their spirits up and while away the time. The handmaidens readily agreed to Medea's plan.

Argos left his brothers keeping watch and returned to the ship. When they witnessed Medea leaving the city, the brothers ran down to the ship to inform Argos of her departure. Argos pulled Jason quickly to his side, to take him to the temple of Hecate. Mopsus went with them to offer his assistance with any oracles they might hear, either on their journey or when they got there. It was just as well he did because along the path stood a shrine next to a poplar tree, where a crow clapped its wings and began to speak in a language only Mopsus could interpret. The bird told Mopsus that Jason must go on alone to meet Medea, so he and Argos held back, telling Jason they would wait and not to worry because Hera watched over him. Jason walked on alone.

Singing could not calm Medea's nerves. Her eyes wandered to the path whenever she thought she heard footsteps. After frequent false alarms, Jason finally appeared, striding purposefully forward. Medea stood transfixed, blushing intensely and almost blinded by the sight of the hero marching towards her. Still she could not move when Jason arrived and faced her, despite the handmaidens stepping back to give them room.

Jason told Medea that she had no need to be afraid of him, and that he needed her help. He added that if he succeeded and returned safely with his crew, she would be a heroine to all Greece, and would receive the thanks of the gods. Medea did not answer, but instead handed over the potion, much to the delight of Jason. After another soulful pause, Medea finally addressed the man with whom she was completely obsessed. The potion only worked if Jason followed her strict instructions, she told him. When he received the dragon's teeth from Aeëtes, he was to bathe at midnight in the stream of the nearby sacred river. Then, without any witnesses, he should dig a round pit in which he was to sacrifice a ewe to Hecate. After his dedication, Jason must cover himself in honey then retreat from the sacrificial pyre without looking back. At dawn, he must apply the potion all over. If he did all that, Jason would be like a god, impervious to spears and flame, but only for one day. Medea continued that when he sowed the dragon's teeth and the earthbound warriors sprang up, Jason should throw a large rock among them so that they would fight among themselves. Jason would then be free to take the Fleece and return home.

Medea had one more request: she asked Jason to remember her even though he would be far away, wherever he may be. Jason replied that of course he would, but that he hoped Aeëtes would come around to becoming friends for her sake. That was not the answer Medea was looking for. She scoffed at Jason's optimism regarding her father, then promised that she would find out if he forgot her, and visit him in Iolcus to remind him who was responsible for his survival.

Jason hastened to reassure Medea that she would be treated like a goddess by the Greeks for bringing their people home. Besides, Jason noted, if she came to Greece it would be as his wife, to be parted only by death. In that moment, Medea knew that Jason felt about her as she did about him, and the two star-crossed lovers fell silent, lost in the moment. Jason broke their reverie, pointing out that the day was fading and that Medea needed to return to the palace, in case someone should ask where she had been.

Medea called her handmaidens and then, mounting her chariot, sped home where she sat deep in thought of both the trials to come and her impending treachery. Jason returned to Mopsus and Argos and told them what had happened as they walked back to the ship. When he showed the Argonauts the potion and told them the story, they celebrated into the night, except for Idas who sat apart, still brooding.

The following morning, Telamon and Aethalides left for the palace to collect the dragon's teeth. Jason, meanwhile, prepared to carry out Medea's instructions that night, so that when the sun went down and the Argonauts prepared for bed, he snuck away, carrying a sheep brought by Argos for the sacrifice. Jason bathed in the sacred river before digging a pit in a nearby meadow and filling it with wood. He then sacrificed the sheep, placed it on the fire, and poured on the libations.

(Opposite) A shot of Tim Severin's crew as they row their modern *Argo*. (Top Foto)

Having completed the rituals, Jason called on Hecate and began to walk back to the ship. Hecate appeared behind him, bathed in bright light and surrounded by snakes. Hellish noises ripped through the night, and the ground quivered, but Jason would not look back. Arriving at the *Argo* just as dawn was breaking, Jason had no time for rest; he needed to get ready, for today was the day he would retrieve the Golden Fleece.

The Trials of Jason

For Aeëtes, today was the day he would have his revenge on the Greek pirates. The king dressed as for war and presented an awesome sight to his gathered subjects. His four-plumed helmet gleamed in the sun as Aeëtes picked up his heavy shield and spear before mounting his chariot and taking the reins. The king then led his people down the road to the Plain of Ares.

Back at the *Argo*, Jason steeled himself in preparation for the challenges ahead. He submerged Medea's potion in water then liberally sprinkled the solution over his spear, sword, and shield. The still-sceptical Idas walked over and slashed the spear with his sword but recoiled in pain when it failed to

Jason (Todd Armstrong) battles the earthborn men in the 1963 movie. Despite the enduring popularity of this scene, the original sources clearly state that the earthborn men are creatures of flesh and blood. (Pictorial Press Ltd / Alamy)

make a dent. Jason next drizzled the solution over his body, feeling the strength course immediately through his limbs, swelling his arms and legs with energy. Delighting in his newfound power, Jason tossed his spear and shield in the air and leaped to catch them before joining his crew. The Argonauts stood in wonder, then ran to their oars to take their leader up the river to the Plain of Ares, where he would face the terrible bulls. They arrived on the far shore where Aeëtes waited on the riverbank, the Colchian host ranged behind him on the high ground.

Jason could barely contain himself, and jumped down from the *Argo* as soon as the crew tied her to the shore. His sword hung on a strap over his head, so that in one hand he could carry his spear and shield, while the other was free to pick up the helmet containing the dragon's teeth. Jason looked across the field, where he could see the heavy yoke but, as yet, no bulls. He strode on to the plain and first thrust his spear butt into the ground, took off his helmet and leaned it on the spear, then paced the ground nearby, tracking the lines of hoof prints there. Seemingly lost in thought, Jason just had time to pull his shield around for protection when the bulls emerged from their pen and charged across the plain. The massive beasts thundered forward, their powerful muscles rippling, and bronze hooves shaking the ground. Flame shot out of the bulls' nostrils, creating shimmering heatwaves in the still air. Jason had barely taken his defensive stance when the terrible beasts were upon him.

Jason's curved shield deflected the bulls' razor-sharp horns and flaming breath. Bursts of fire licked around the young leader of the Argonauts, but Medea's potion blocked their burning heat. Then Jason grabbed the horns of one bull, forcing its head down until the animal had to kneel. The other bull renewed its efforts to destroy the defiant man, until Jason brought it down too, with one hard blow. With both animals in positions of submission, Jason threw his shield down, holding them tightly as Castor and Polydeuces rushed over with the yoke, which he bound to the bulls. Jason then attached the guiding pole to the yoke, put his shield on his back, and picked up his spear and the helmet filled with the dragon's teeth.

Prodding the bulls with his spear to get them moving, and ignoring their raging bellows of flame, Jason took charge of the plow. He walked calmly along behind the unhappy animals, casting the teeth out into the new furrows, all the while checking behind him to make sure none of the earthborn warriors sprouted prematurely.

When he finished plowing, Jason released the subdued bulls and sent them back across the plain with a wave of his hand. He gathered his equipment and walked over to where the *Argo* was tied up, still keeping his eye on the plowed field for the first earthborn soldiers to emerge. The Argonauts gathered round to cheer for Jason, who filled his helmet from the river to quench his thirst.

By now, double-pointed spears had started to rise from the soil all across the plain, followed by shining bronze helmets and shields. Jason flexed his muscles and let out a huge roar. He then picked up a nearby boulder and tossed it across the plain into a crowd of now fully emerged earthborn. Jason crouched behind his shield and waited for the soldiers to react. The effects of the boulder did not take long; those earthborn already out of the ground rushed in on each other with spears lowered, while others desperately clawed at the earth trying to get out. Jason seized his chance, leaping from behind his shield, sword in hand, and hacking indiscriminately at the distracted creatures. He caught some earthborn half-emerged and slashed their shoulders and sides; others he sliced through their bellies until the plowed furrows ran deep with earthborn blood. On and on the slaughter went, until there were no more earthborn to kill.

When it was all over King Aeëtes stood in mute shock and anguish at the carnage wrought by Jason, but for the moment he could do nothing. He signalled the Colchians to return to the city, where he would consider his next move.

The Golden Fleece

Guilt crashed down upon Medea when she returned to her chambers. Elsewhere in the palace, Aeëtes was meeting with his army officers, raging at his misfortune and plotting revenge. Medea, however, was on her own, quaking with fear that her assistance to Jason might have been discovered. She tore at her hair, groaning with despair, and, in her darkest moments, she again contemplated suicide. Once more, Hera intervened, suggesting with thoughts that Medea steal away with Argos and his brothers instead. Medea suddenly calmed down in response, resolving to run. She kissed her bed and doors and stroked the walls before pulling out some of her hair to leave on her bed as a memento for her mother. Then Medea fled into the night.

Medea ran through the palace grounds, holding her robe like a veil in one hand, while the other gripped the hem of her tunic. She passed unnoticed under the city watchtowers, then out into the country. Moonlight guided Medea's steps as she raced down to the riverbank. When she got there, she could see the fire on the opposite bank made by the celebrating Argonauts. She called out for Phrontis, the youngest of her four nephews. He heard her, as did Jason, who gathered the Argonauts to search across the river for Medea. She called out twice more to guide her rescuers until, out of the darkness, she could see the boat looming over her. Jason jumped down, followed by Phrontis and Argos even before the crew had tied the *Argo* to the shore.

Medea fell to her knees, begging them to save her from Aeëtes, and to save themselves too, because the king surely knew everything. They had to act quickly though, she continued, and retrieve the Fleece before Aeëtes mounted a hunt for them. She would help calm the serpent that protected the Fleece, so that Jason could snatch his prize and get away unharmed, but she demanded that he honor his promises to her. He must not make her a byword for treason and dishonor. Jason took Medea in his arms and raised her up, telling her once again that he would marry her once they returned safely to Greece.

Aware that time was of the essence, Jason lifted Medea on board the *Argo* and ordered the crew to row to the sacred grove. At dawn they arrived at a soot-blackened altar to Zeus, where a path led up into the trees.

Jason and Medea flitted along the path until they could see the great oak tree from which hung the Golden Fleece. Under the tree, however, two unblinking, monstrous eyes watched the would-be thieves arrive. They belonged to the serpent of the grove, and it slowly uncoiled itself, unleashing a tremendous hissing into the cool morning air. The serpent raised itself up as if to strike until Medea stepped forward and began to sing. The enchanting song affected the serpent immediately. Jason, following fearfully behind Medea, saw the monster visibly relax and begin to descend; yet its eyes never wandered in their gaze until Medea took a sprig of juniper, dipped it into the potion she had brought along, and sprinkled it over the serpent's face. Finally, the monster's jaw slumped down in a slumber that soon spread through its coils. Medea signalled Jason to come forward.

Medea feeds drugged fruit to the dragon, while Jason grabs the Golden Fleece in this scene from a second-century CE Roman sarcophagus. (Cesi Collection; Boncompagni Ludovisi Collection)

Jason (Todd Armstrong) battles the dragon that guards the Golden Fleece in the 1963 movie. The movie borrowed from other Greek myths to get its multi-headed dragon. (Photos 12 / Alamy)

Jason needed no second invitation; he snatched the Golden Fleece from the oak, then withdrew quickly past Medea. While Jason carried out his raid, Medea rubbed more potion over the serpent's head to keep it calm. She stopped when Jason reached a safe distance and called for her to leave the sacred grove. The monster slumbered on as the couple stole away, Jason hauling the heavy Fleece over his left shoulder. With the Fleece trailing down his back down to his ankles, Jason appeared to shimmer and shine, while he held on tightly to the wondrous object in fear that he should ever lose it.

The Argonauts marvelled at the sight of Jason and Medea approaching hand-in-hand in a golden cloud. They reached to take the Fleece from him, but he held it back while he boarded the *Argo*. On his way toward the rear of the ship, Jason placed the Fleece on a mantle and made sure Medea was seated comfortably; then he addressed the crew. The object of their mission was now in safe hands, he told them, and they must now return to Greece, where Jason had promised to marry Medea.

The Argonauts must protect her, he continued, for she had saved them from defeat and embarrassment. Finally, he warned them that Aeëtes would surely block the river mouth and they would have to run the Colchian gauntlet: half of them must row while the rest hold their shields up to deter missiles. When he finished, Jason dressed in his war armor, drew his sword, and cut through the ropes tying the *Argo* to the riverbank. With Medea at his side, Jason signalled the Argonauts to pull away.

Book IV: The Journey Home

The Wrathful King

Aeëtes quickly discovered Medea's treachery and the loss of the Golden Fleece. The king was angered, and ordered the Colchians to gather their weapons and armor, and muster at the assembly grounds. Aeëtes mounted his chariot, holding his curved shield in his left hand and a large pine torch in his right, and addressed the gathered soldiers. He exhorted his people to bring back Medea so that he could extract his vengeance on her, and warned that they should give up their lives if necessary, or they would face his wrath. Aeëtes led the charge down to the river, with his son, Apsyrtus, driving his chariot.

The Colchian troops rushed along the riverbanks, but the Argonauts were already past the breakwater, pulling on the *Argo*'s oars for all they were worth. Undaunted, the Colchians boarded their ships and continued the pursuit out to sea. Even as the Argonauts hoisted their sail, they could see the Colchian boats spreading out like a flock of maddened birds in angry flight.

Fortunately for the Argonauts, Hera was on their side. She urged the wind to blow favorably, so that, by the third morning out of Colchis, the *Argo* was well ahead of the pursuit when it reached the mouth of the River Halys, in the land of the Paphlagonians. Medea told Jason to build an altar to Hecate on the shore, and he also took this opportunity to discuss with his crew their voyage home. The prophecy of Phineas that they should return by a different route guided their thoughts, but none of them were quite sure what the old man had meant. Argus, the ship builder, spoke first. He recommended that they sail to Orchomenus, as foretold by Phineas. From there, they should try and find the River Ister and navigate it until they came to the Trinaerian Sea, and from there on to Greece.

The Argonauts were considering Argus's suggestion when suddenly they saw a trail of light in the sky—which they deemed a sign from Hera—and decided to follow it. They set sail immediately and headed back out to sea. Before long, the Argonauts sighted the mouth of the River Ister. They dropped sail and prepared to enter.

The Colchians, meanwhile, had spread their net wide to track down the *Argo*. Some went to Pontus and down into the Hellespont; others, led by Apsyrtus, sailed up the River Ister. When they reached an island called Peuce

(Overleaf) Jason and Medea take the Golden Fleece. In most versions of the story, Medea uses her enchantments to put the guardian of the Golden Fleece to sleep. Only in later stories did Jason fight the dragon.

that split the river in two, the Colchians took the lower course, not knowing that the Argonauts rowed along the upper river. Apsyrtus therefore reached the Sea of Cronus first, allowing him to cut all the exits through which the *Argo* might escape.

Jason reached two islands near the mouth of the river, on one of which sat a temple to Artemis. Realizing the Colchians surrounded him, Jason chose to land. The Argonauts gathered, and reasoned that they would likely lose in a fight to the Colchians; therefore, they had little choice but to hold a conference with Apsyrtus and his heralds to debate the available options. At the subsequent meeting between the two sides, it was decided that the Argonauts could keep the Fleece because Aeëtes had promised it to them. As for Medea, the Argonauts agreed she should be placed in the temple of Artemis until a decision was made to either allow her to continue or send her back to face the king.

Medea listened to the debate with growing alarm. After it concluded, she pulled Jason aside and led him out of earshot of his crew. When they were alone, Medea turned on Jason, accusing him of forgetting his promises, and reminding him of all the sacrifices she had made so that he could get the Fleece; she had given up her family and sold her honor as a woman to follow him and become his wife, and he must stand by her now in her time of need. The alternative for her, she added, was surely torture and death, and if that lay in her future she cursed him to fall foul of the gods, lose the Fleece, and be driven from Greece by the Furies.

Jason drew back at the vehemence of Medea's words. He replied that the situation was perilous; enemies surrounded them and the native tribes would help Apsyrtus, but, if she followed his plan, he would see to her safety by getting rid of Apsyrtus then fighting through the leaderless Colchians if necessary. Jason's speech calmed Medea. She now acknowledged her role in the Argonauts's predicament, so offered to lure her brother Apsyrtus into the trap if Jason would protect her from the Colchians. It was up to him, she said, to kill Apsyrtus and fight the Colchians.

Jason's Shameful Act

Agreed on their scheme, Medea and Jason organized a collection of gifts for the Colchian heralds, including the sacred crimson robe that had belonged to Hypsipyle of Lemnos. Medea persuaded them to have her brother attend when she arrived at the temple of Artemis, on the grounds that she had been kidnapped by the Argonauts and had a plan to escape with the Fleece back to Aeëtes. That night, the Argonauts dropped Medea off on the island and sailed away. Jason was not with them, because he had hidden himself near the Temple. Apsyrtus arrived soon afterwards to conspire with Medea. Barely had they finished talking, however, when Jason leaped out sword in hand from behind his cover. Medea drew her veil down across her eyes to avoid watching the fate of Apsyrtus, but Jason did not blink, thrusting his blade deep into the Colchian prince.

Apsyrtus staggered into the vestibule of the temple where he filled his cupped hands with blood then wiped them on Medea's robe as she tried to get away. Jason moved in on Apsyrtus to finish him, then drank from the dead man's blood three times and spat it out each time, in a traditional ritual carried out by murderers seeking absolution. The gods, however, had witnessed Jason's desecration of the Temple of Artemis, and they were furious.

Medea was up and running even as her brother lay dying. She grabbed a torch and lit it as a signal to the Argonauts out in the bay. Jason's crew were already dressed for war and primed at their oars. The *Argo* shot forward until it lay alongside the nearest Colchian ship. The stunned Colchian crew had little chance of surviving the whirlwind of bronze-clad warriors that descended on them, hacking and slashing through bone and flesh until, finally, the carnage was over.

Now that their escape route lay unimpeded, the Argonauts drew together with Medea and Jason to decide on how to proceed. Peleus argued that they must embark immediately and get away from the rest of the Colchians. They would not follow, he added, because without a leader the Colchians would fall out among themselves. The Argonauts took Peleus's advice and rowed quickly but stealthily away until they reached the island of Electra near the River Eridanus. Peleus was wrong, however, because the enraged Colchians wanted to continue their mission and avenge their leader. Only Hera's intervention with bolts of lightning prevented them from giving chase.

The Death of Apsyrtus by Herbert Draper. In one version of the story of the Golden Fleece, Medea takes her brother Apsyrtus onto the *Argo* as a hostage. When she sees her father's pursuing ships, she chops her brother into pieces and throws the pieces into the ocean. The Argonauts then escape while Aeëtes stops to pick up the pieces. In another version, the Argonauts turn around and defeat the Colchians in a pitched battle. (Ivy Close Images / Alamy)

Fearing Aeëtes's wrath, and with nowhere else to go, the Colchians decided to stay in the lands surrounding them and disembarked. On the Argonauts sailed to the land of the Hylleans, with no idea of the Colchian drama left in their wake. Nor had they any clue about the trials an angry Zeus had planned for them.

Divine Punishment

The killing of Apsyrtus enraged Zeus, who proclaimed that the Argonauts could not return to Greece unpunished. They must instead seek the counsel of the sorceress Circe, who lived on the island of Aeaea, if they were to expunge the guilt of Jason's terrible deed. The unwitting crew pushed on away from the Hyllean lands, and down to Corcyra. From there, the *Argo* sailed past Melite, with none of the crew realizing how endless their voyage promised to be if they did not go to Aeaea.

Hera could not sit idly by, however; so she gathered a storm that sent the *Argo* spinning back to the island of Electra. Then Hera spoke to the Argonauts through the beam of the ship, which Athena had provided at the start of their quest. She told the thoroughly terrified Argonauts of Zeus's fury at the murder of Apsyrtus. Hera then commanded Castor and Polydeuces to pray to the gods for a path through the Ausonian Sea and on to where Circe waited.

Hera's pronouncement stunned the Argonauts, but they had no option other than to follow her instructions. The twins therefore beseeched the gods for guidance, while the rest of the crew rigged the sail to continue the voyage. They sailed along a stream of the River Eridanus, which soon opened out into a deep, dark, foul-smelling lake of the same name. At the other end of the lake, the *Argo* drew into the River Rhodanus, which flowed into the Ionian and Sardinian seas, among others. The Argonauts cruised down the Rhodanus into the stormy lakes that linked up through the numerous lands of the Celts.

At one point, the Argonauts grew confused about which way to go and nearly took a disastrous turn, only for Hera to head them off with an almighty screech that diverted the fearful Argonauts back to the correct path. Hera also surrounded the *Argo* with mist to ease its passage through the territory of the warlike Celts. Clearing that danger, the Argonauts reached the Stoechades islands, then navigated along the Tyrrhenian shores of Ausonia until they finally came to Aeaea.

Circe

Scarcely had the Argonauts secured their ship to the shore of Aeaea than they saw the sorceress washing her hair and clothes in the spray of the sea. Spellbound, they watched as Circe came toward them, trailed by a mass of shapeless monsters. She extended her hand and gestured for the warriors to follow her, but Jason ordered them to stay; only he and Medea would go to face whatever fate Circe had in mind for them. The couple walked calmly along the track left by Circe

Another major source for the story of Jason and the Argonauts is the *Orphic Argonautica*, a poem, probably composed in the fourth century CE. This poem is narrated by Orpheus and places a much bigger emphasis on the deeds of the musician. (Ivy Close Images / Alamy)

until they reached the sorceress's hall. Circe was waiting, and ordered Jason and Medea to sit on brightly burnished seats by the hearth. Neither looked Circe in the eyes, Medea going so far as to hide her face in her hands, while Jason fixed his stare on his sword that he placed between himself and the sorceress.

Circe immediately recognized the guilt of Jason and Medea, and began the rituals that would cleanse them of their crimes. She sacrificed a newborn piglet, and drizzled its blood on their hands while calling on Zeus to hear her prayer, then prepared drinks and cakes to appease the gods and keep the Furies away from the couple. With the ritual complete, Circe sat opposite Jason and Medea. Recognizing a kindred spirit in the younger sorceress, Circe asked them about their journey and why they had come to her island asking for help.

Medea told almost the whole story, leaving out the murder of Apsyrtus, but Circe had already guessed at the hidden truth of Medea's guilt. Circe chastised Medea for this shameful deed of which she would never approve, adding that Aeëtes would not rest in his thirst for revenge, even if that meant going to Greece. With that, Circe dismissed Medea from her presence, telling her to take Jason with her. Medea was inconsolable at Circe's rant, so it was left to Jason to take her hand and lead Medea away from Circe's home.

The couple picked their way back to the *Argo*, but their leaving Circe's hall had been noted by Iris, a messenger of Hera, who quickly returned to the goddess to make her report.

Hera had work to do if she was to help Jason reach his homeland safely. When Iris returned, Hera told her to ask Thetis, the water nymph, to come and see her, and then to tell Hephaestus, whose forge stood on a nearby beach, to hold off the blasts from his fires and let the *Argo* pass. From there, Iris was to ask Aeolus, ruler of the winds, to cease all winds except for the west wind, so that the Argonauts could reach the island of Alcinous unmolested. Iris sprang into action and delivered her messages. Hephaestus and Aeolus agreed to Hera's requests, and Thetis soon arrived at Olympus, where Hera had specific instructions for her.

Thetis listened while Hera told her of Jason's voyage so far and how he would need more help to get through the trials still to come. The winds and fires of Hephaestus's forge had already been taken care of, Hera continued, but she wanted Thetis and her sisters, the Nereids, to assist the *Argo* through the twin horrors of Scylla and Charybdis.

Thetis readily acceded to Hera's request, and dived into the sea to meet with her sisters. When she had explained the plan and sent them out to the Ausonian Sea to make ready, Thetis swam in the blink of an eye to where the Argonauts rested on the beach. She picked out Peleus, her husband, and silently touched his hand to draw his attention. Thetis spoke softly, telling Peleus that the *Argo* must sail at dawn, and that her sisters waited to guide the ship past Scylla and Charybdis, and then through the treacherous wandering rocks known as the Planctae. However, Peleus was to inform no one of her assistance when it happened. Thetis left as quickly and silently as she came, leaving a breathless Peleus to tell the crew to be ready to sail at dawn.

Sirens

It was with renewed vigor that the Argonauts got their ship ready the next morning. They drew up the anchor, cast off the hawsers, and ran up the sail just in time for the west wind to spring up and pull it taut along the crossbeam. The *Argo* made good time, and the Argonauts soon arrived off the island of Anthemoessa, where a strange, beguiling song greeted them across the waves.

This was the island of the Sirens, the daughters of the river god Achelous, who bewitched unwary sailors to wreck their ships on the rocks surrounding the island. The Argonauts were set to be the latest victims of the siren song when Orpheus, realizing the terrible danger they were in, sang a melody that brought his shipmates to their senses. In the nick of time, the Argonauts pulled the *Argo* away to the west; too late for Butes, however, who was overcome by the siren song and jumped overboard to swim ashore. There was nothing the distraught Argonauts could do to save their young shipmate, however, so they sailed on in silence.

Scylla and Charybdis

The Argonauts had little time to reflect on their loss because looming ahead, in a narrow strait, lay the twin perils of Scylla and Charybdis. On one side of the strait, the smooth rock face of Scylla promised to shatter ships that came too close; on the other side, the whirlpool Charybdis sucked into the abyss anything nearing its deadly maw.

Smoke and fog, illuminated by bursts of fire from nearby mountains, filled the dreadful scene in front of the *Argo*, making certain navigation impossible. Just when the *Argo* set off, however, Thetis and the Nereids rose to the surface to help guide the ship. Thetis grabbed hold of the rudder blade and began to steer the *Argo*, while the Nereids circled around, raising the spirits of the surrounded Argonauts.

With the help of Thetis and the Nereids, the *Argo* forged a path between the twin hazards, and on towards the Planctae beyond. The Nereids kept the wandering rocks away from the hull as the ship navigated the treacherous waters until, finally, the ship was through and again heading west. Hera looked on, overjoyed, and hugged Athena when the danger had passed. Jason and his hugely relieved Argonauts celebrated too, and the *Argo* sailed on.

Orpheus saves (most) of the Argonauts from the deadly song of the Sirens.

Return of the Colchians

The Argonauts soon sailed into the Ionian gulf and came to the island of Drepane, where Alcinous, King of the Phaeacians, and his queen Arete prepared a welcome as if the Argonauts were their own sons returning from a dangerous adventure. Jason's crew revelled in the celebrations, but their joy was cut short by the arrival of a new Colchian army intent on seizing Medea. Alcinous moved quickly between the two sides, hoping to prevent all-out war on his island. Medea, meanwhile, begged Arete to protect her and not hand her over to the horrible fate she expected at the hands of Aeëtes.

Turning to the Argonauts, Medea reminded them of everything she had lost so that they could capture the Fleece and return safely to their families, and that if they betrayed her now they should live in fear of the gods for the rest of their lives. The warriors drew their swords and brandished spears and swore to protect Medea, but darkness fell before either side came to blows. All slept, except Medea who fretted long into the night.

Alcinous and his queen also had trouble sleeping. They lay in the dark, discussing how to deal with Medea. Arete pleaded with her husband to save Medea, partly on the prudent grounds that the Argonauts lived closer than the Colchians and it would be easier for them to exact their revenge, and partly because of Medea's begging Arete for help. Moreover, she added, Jason was committed to marrying Medea and that was a better fate than the vengeance of her father. Alcinous in reply pointed out that Aeëtes was a great warlord and quite capable of attacking the Greeks. If Medea was still a virgin, he continued, she must be sent back to her father, but if she was married or pregnant then she should stay with her husband. Having made his decision, the king rolled over to sleep.

Arete lay awake a little longer before rising to quietly summon a messenger to go to Jason and tell him that he must marry Medea immediately.

Arete's herald reached Jason, who was surrounded by watchful Argonauts wearing full armor. The warriors rejoiced when they heard the herald's story, and quickly set about organizing the sacrifices necessary for a successful wedding. Some of them took the Fleece to a sacred cave nearby and laid it out to make a splendid wedding bed. Nymphs sent by Hera brought garlands of flowers to spread around the cave. Finally, the nymphs unrolled fine linen to complete the marriage bed. The Argonauts took up defensive positions at the cave's entrance and Orpheus began to play the marriage song. Jason and Medea arrived soon after, and became man and wife, but even in their happiness they feared the judgement of Alcinous.

Dawn broke the next morning with all parties already awake in anticipation of the drama to come. Alcinous left the city carrying his golden staff of justice, accompanied by his army in full war panoply. Crowds gathered along the way, brought out by the news spread around the island by Hera, and the

(Opposite) The *Argo* squeezes through the wandering rocks. (Mary Evans Picture Library / Alamy)

JASON AND THE MOVIES

The story of Jason and the Argonauts has been dramatized twice in the modern era. The first effort came in 1963 when director Don Chaffey and renowned special effects creator Ray Harryhausen combined to make a movie starring Todd Armstrong as Jason and Nancy Kovack as Medea. The movie was neither a hit nor failure at the box office but, primarily as a result of Harryhausen's spectacular stop-motion animation, it has since become the most popular and readily identifiable rendition of the Golden Fleece story.

There are a number of significant differences, however, between the movie and the classical version as told by Apollonius. The most notable are the enhanced role of Talos and his relocation in the narrative, and the dragon's teeth soldiers who become skeletons in the movie and chase Jason across the landscape rather than fight amongst themselves when Jason throws the rock into their midst.

The second movie version was the lavish 2000 made-for-television movie starring Jason London as Jason and Jolene Blalock as Medea. The movie was directed by Nick Willing and featured CGI special effects for the monsters. This version is more faithful to the original legend and incorporates elements of Valerius Flaccus's retelling, including the fight with the sea monster and the inclusion of Atalanta in the crew; although her efforts to seduce Jason are a modern inclusion, as is the killing of Pelias that concludes the movie.

The recent video game, *Rise of the Argonauts*, departs further from the myth, with the Fleece being sought to heal Jason's dying wife.

Jason (Jason London) and Medea (Jolene Blalock) in the 2000 made-for-television film. (AF archive/Alamy)

air crackled with tension. Some of the Phaeacian men sacrificed a sheep and cow, while women brought linen and gold ornaments for the newlyweds. The nymphs danced and sang in honor of Hera.

Alcinous had heard of the marriage and kept to his word that Medea would not be returned to the Colchians. Like their counterparts before them, the Colchians dreaded returning to face Aeëtes. They begged Alcinous to let them stay on the island as Phaeacians, to which he agreed. Turning to the Argonauts, the king wished them a successful voyage home, and gave them many gifts, including twelve handmaidens to serve Medea. A week after their arrival, the Argonauts sailed away from Drepane on a fresh breeze, hoping their next stop would be home. Their destination was not Greece, however, but Libya.

THE ENDLESS DESERT

The *Argo* sped on with full sail, past the land of the Curetes, through the Echinades islands, and on to the land of Pelops. Then a north wind blew up to tug the ship towards the Libyan Sea. For nine days and nights the Argonauts fought against the storm's inexorable force, but could not stop the *Argo* from being pulled deeper into the Gulf of Syrtis. Once in the gulf, there was no way out because of the shifting, sandy shoals and impenetrable beds of seaweed. Ahead lay the hostile, desolate Libyan desert, and it was on to that shore that the *Argo* came to rest.

The Argonauts climbed down from the decks and looked around in dismay bordering on outright despair. Search parties sent along the beach to find a way out returned with no hope for the desperate crew. When darkness fell, the Argonauts rolled into their blankets, fearing they might be dead by morning, while Medea and her handmaidens wailed laments deep into the night. Fortunately, the nymphs of the desert took pity on the abandoned sailors.

Jason was lying with his cloak over his head when the nymphs appeared beside him. One pulled his cloak off and chastised Jason for abandoning hope. She assured him that he would get back to Greece if he paid attention to a significant omen that was about to happen. The nymphs vanished before he could reply, but Jason felt renewed and quickly woke up his shipmates. The downcast Argonauts gathered round to hear Jason speak. He told them of the nymphs and their cryptic message. Then, just as Jason finished, a huge horse rose out of the surf, shook out the spray from its golden mane, and galloped off into the sands.

Peleus understood immediately the meaning of this incredible event, and shouted to the Argonauts that they must carry the ship on their shoulders through the desert, following the hoof-prints of the magical horse. The warriors sprang into action, preparing the *Argo* for her new voyage, then hoisted her on their shoulders.

The Argonauts marched across the blistering desert for twelve days and nights, until they came to the Tritonian Lake. They did not stop, but strode in until the waters buoyed the *Argo,* making it float, and only then did the Argonauts release their burden. The starving and thirsty sailors could not rest, however, because they needed to hunt for food and water. They set off along the shore, where they arrived at the garden of Atlas with its golden apple trees.

The Argonauts saw nymphs, the Hesperides, in among the trees, dancing and chanting songs, but when they approached the nymphs dissolved into the earth. Orpheus called on them to come back and show the Argonauts where they could find a spring. The nymphs returned out of the ground in the form of trees. One of them, Aegle, spoke, accusing the Argonauts of bringing Heracles with them. She continued that Heracles had visited the garden the previous day, killed their guardian serpent, and then smashed a rock to create the spring to which she pointed.

The strangeness of the nymph's story did not deter the Argonauts from flocking to the spring and slaking their thirst, though some hoped that they might meet Heracles again on their way home. After gorging themselves on fresh water, the Argonauts split up to search for Heracles. Calaïs and Zetes took to the air while Euphemus sprinted out into the desert. Lynceus used his far-sightedness to scan the horizons, and Canthus followed along, hoping to find answers from Heracles on what had happened to his friend Polyphemus. The search was in vain, however, and the Argonauts returned to the ship, all except for Canthus whose terrible fate soon became apparent.

The Deaths of Canthus and Mopsus

For a man who lived as a hero, Canthus died in a most prosaic fashion. While out on his search for Heracles, he came across a flock of sheep and quickly decided to take some back for his shipmates. The shepherd had other ideas and, throwing a well-aimed slingshot, killed Canthus. The unfortunate shepherd died too, at the hands of the avenging Argonauts when they discovered Canthus's fate. They buried Canthus and took the sheep for which he had sacrificed his life.

Death had not finished with the Argonauts this day, however. As they returned to the ship, Mopsus stood on the tail of a snake lying in the sand, causing it to whip back and bite the man's leg. The snake's poison immediately took effect, numbing the Argonaut's body before its fatal last spasm. Jason and the other Argonauts grieved for their comrade and built a burial mound over his body, befitting his heroic status.

It was with heavy hearts that the crew boarded the *Argo* for the next leg of their journey.

The Tritonian Lake

The *Argo* sailed out into the Tritonian Lake on the edge of a southerly breeze. The Argonauts lacked direction, however, and could not find an exit to the ocean. With mounting frustration amongst its crew, the little ship meandered around aimlessly until Orpheus called for Jason to steer into shore. His plan was to make an offering to the gods in exchange for a path through to the sea. The sailors disembarked and conducted the ritual, and straight away Triton, the son of Poseidon, appeared. He introduced himself and offered a clod of earth to Euphemus.

(Overleaf) Talos, the Bronze Man. According to various myths, Talos was created by either the god Hephaestus, or the inventor Daedalus, in order to guard Europa (a woman favored by Zeus). Talos walked around the island of Crete three times a day, throwing rocks at any enemies that might approach.

Triton listened while Euphemus explained how they came to be in this predicament, then stretched out his hand to show them the path they must sail. Once in the ocean, he added, they should stay close to the coast until they reached a cape, then head straight out to sea to get home.

The Argonauts scrambled on board, eager to get underway. They did not see Triton enter the water behind them but nevertheless urged Jason to sacrifice their best sheep to him, which he promptly did by cutting its throat and throwing it over the stern. Triton was delighted and appeared to the Argonauts in his true form as half-man, half-sea serpent. He took up a position in front of the *Argo* and guided the ship out to the ocean where he disappeared under the waves.

The exuberant Argonauts spent the evening in the bay then sailed on at dawn the following morning, keeping the desert on their left. The Argonauts saw the headland receding, then a south wind carried them forward out to sea. When the wind died, they took to their oars, heading directly for Crete. But there a new danger awaited them.

Talos, the Bronze Man

The island of Crete was protected in unique fashion by a bronze giant called Talos. His armored skin was invulnerable to mortal weapons, so that when the Argonauts tried to tie up on the shore Talos easily drove them away by throwing rocks. The Argonauts drew back the *Argo* to a safe range while they considered their options. What the Argonauts did not know was that Talos was created with a weak point on his ankle, where a lightly covered vein presented a life-threatening target.

It was Medea who stepped forward, ordering the Argonauts to stay out of range while she dealt with the problem. The crew watched in fascination as Medea began to chant ritual incantations that conjured death-spirits from Hades. She kneeled, fastening her stare on Talos's eyes, all the while praying and singing in a furious temper before unleashing phantom demons against the bronze giant. Talos responded with greater efforts at throwing rocks, straining to sink the *Argo*.

The giant's obsession proved his downfall when, distracted, he caught his ankle on a pointed boulder that ripped open his exposed vein. Talos's molten blood poured out on to the sand, and he staggered for a few moments, growing weaker by the second, until, finally, he crashed to the ground. The jubilant Argonauts rode ashore in safety and, before they sailed the next morning, set up a shrine to Athena for their deliverance.

Darkness and Light

The *Argo* sailed all that day and into the night, but the Argonauts grew increasingly fearful when the stars and moon did not show to help them navigate. The chaos of darkness sent the sailors into new fits of anguish, and

This relief illustrates the tragic life of Medea after the quest for the Golden Fleece, which is most famously related in the play *Medea* by Euripides.

some even wondered if they were alive or dead. Finally, Jason held out his hands and called on Apollo, as god of the sun, to save them. Straight away, Apollo came down to the Melantian rocks, from which he held up his silver bow and cast a beam of light out to sea. The Argonauts could now see the tiny island of Hippuris and rowed quickly across to drop anchor. Dawn came soon after and the hugely relieved Argonauts built an altar to Apollo.

The Argonauts sailed on, passing along the coast of Greece without further incident until they came to the beach of Pagasae. Jason's epic adventure to recover the Golden Fleece and return to claim his kingdom was nearly over.

The Return to Iolcus

For a couple whose love burned so brightly and who had overcome such adversity, Jason and Medea's lives after the search for the Golden Fleece disintegrated into tragedy. When they arrived in Iolcus, Medea persuaded the usurper Pelias's daughters that they could help rejuvenate their father by chopping him into pieces and placing his parts into a cauldron with some magical herbs. They quickly followed Medea's recommendation, but too late they realized their role in regicide—the murder of the king—when Medea withheld the required herbs.

Pelias's son, Acastus, had seen the murder, however, and promptly drove Medea and Jason out of Iolcus. From there, the couple moved to Corinth where Medea gave birth to two sons. The idyllic love between Medea and Jason appeared as strong as ever, but then Jason made a fatal error.

For all his promises to Medea, Jason was still the son of a Greek king and she

a foreign princess; it was only right, to Jason anyway, that he should marry into Greek royalty despite his promises of everlasting loyalty to Medea. Therefore, Jason married Glauce, the daughter of King Creon of Corinth, hoping to keep Medea as his mistress. Medea flew into a rage, berating Jason for abandoning her. She could never return to Colchis and no one in Greece would have her, or so she thought. As luck would have it, the king of Athens arrived in Corinth and offered Medea protection if she would use her magic to give him children. Medea now set about plotting a vicious revenge on her unfaithful husband.

Medea paid a call on Jason to apologize for her previous behavior and present a gift of a beautiful dress for Glauce. Jason delightedly took the dress to his new bride. Glauce was obviously enchanted by the dress and decided to wear it for her father to see. But Medea had laced the dress with a poison that burned. When Glauce put on the dress, the poison acted quickly, killing the princess in hideous fashion. Her father died too in his desperate efforts to save Glauce.

In the meantime, Medea killed Jason's children with a knife so that he would be fully punished, then escaped to Athens. Jason did not follow; rather he stayed on until finally linking up with Peleus, who was a prince in his own right, and Telamon. They attacked Iolcus and restored Jason to his kingdom, but Jason had also upset his benefactor goddess Hera when he abandoned Medea.

His misfortunes continued, therefore, until finally a weary Jason fell asleep beside the decaying remains of the *Argo* on the beach, where it had been deserted after the search for the Fleece. While the former hero slept, the rotting stern broke off and killed him, a disgraceful end to a life that would become legend.

GLOSSARY

Beguiling: Using charm or deception to attract the interest of somebody.

Berating: Yelling or scolding somebody in an angry or lengthy way.

Billowed: To move forward pushed by air or gusts of wind.

Bracers: A type of arm- or wristband used as armor.

Brooding: Meditating, pondering, or thinking anxiously about something.

Canon: A widely accepted, authoritative list of books.

Chastised: To criticize or harshly denounce somebody for his or her actions.

Cuirass: A type of plate armor that covers and protects the region between the neck and the waist.

Despotically: As a cruel, ruthless leader with complete control over his or her subjects.

Greaves: A type of armor that protects the shin.

Hawsers: Sturdy, thick ropes used to tie up a ship at harbor.

Hellenistic: Of or relating to Greek culture or history after the reign of Alexander the Great.

Hoplite: A well-armed infantry soldier in ancient Greece.

Impervious: Not affected or subject to the effects of an external factor, such as a weapon or a charm.

Interpolation: The inclusion or addition of new elements into something, particularly into a text.

Isthmus: A narrow strip of land that connects two larger landmasses.

Libations: Liquids or beverages, such as wine, that are poured as an offering to the gods.

Maelstrom: A dangerous, swirling pool of fast-moving waters.

Nocked: Fit an arrow into the string of a bow.

Oracle: A person who served as a channel through which the gods could speak in ancient Greece.

Regicide: The murder of a king or queen.

Rollers: Revolving cylinders that are used to move something otherwise too heavy to move forward.

Treachery: A violation of trust or confidence.

Unanimously: In complete agreement without any disapproval.

Unwary: Gullible or easily fooled, especially due to a low level of alert.

Usurper: One who unrightfully seizes or takes possession of an office or post.

FOR MORE INFORMATION

Center for Hellenic Studies (CHS)
3100 Whitehaven Street NW
Washington, DC 20008
(202) 745-4400
Website: http://chs.harvard.edu
Through its archaeological and research programs, the CHS promotes the
    exploration of ancient Greek culture. It publishes research, hosts a
    discussion series, and grants fellowships for students interested in
    Hellenic studies.

International Association for Comparative Mythology (IACM)
c/o Department of South Asian Studies
Harvard University
1 Bow Street, 3rd floor
Cambridge, MA 02138
(617) 496-2990
Website: http://www.compmyth.org
The IACM promotes the investigation and research of mythologies in
    cultures throughout history, comparing and contrasting the elements
    of different mythological traditions and their places in society. They
    host annual conferences in addition to disseminating articles, books,
    and other educational materials on mythology.

Metropolitan Museum of Art
1000 Fifth Avenue
New York, NY 10028
(212) 650-2335
Website: http://www.metmuseum.org
The Metropolitan Museum of Art hosts twenty-seven galleries of Greek and
    Roman art, including vases, statues, and gemstones. The Met also
    houses over twelve thousand volumes on Greek and Roman art in its
    Onassis Library for Hellenic and Roman Art.

Museum of Classical Antiquities
University of Ottawa
Desmarais Building
55 Laurier Avenue East, 3rd Floor
Ottawa, ON K1N 6N5
Canada

(613) 562-5800, ext. 1650

Website: http://www.cla-srs.uottawa.ca/eng/musee_greco.html

The University of Ottawa's Museum of Classical Antiquities collects,
preserves, and displays pottery, archaeological objects, and artwork
dating back to the seventh century BCE from ancient Greek and
ancient Roman civilizations. Guided tours are available for students of
any age and independent researchers engaged in the antiquities.

Museum of Fine Arts, Boston

Avenue of the Arts

465 Huntington Avenue

Boston, MA 02115

(617) 267-9300

Website: http://www.mfa.org

The Art of the Ancient World collection at the Museum of Fine Arts in
Boston holds over eighty-three thousand works of art from antiquity,
including a vast collection of vases, portraits, and jewelry from ancient
Greece and its Mediterranean surroundings.

Theatre Nefteli

30 Thorncliffe Park Drive

Toronto, ON M4H 1H8

Canada

(416) 425-2485

Website: http://www.theatre-nefeli.com

Founded in 1991 by members of the Greek community of Toronto, Theatre
Nefteli travels and produces plays, dances, and other theatric works
rooted in Greek culture and heritage. They are highly acclaimed for
their modern adaptations of Greek classics.

WEBSITES

Because of the changing nature of Internet links, Rosen Publishing has
developed an online list of websites related to the subject of this book. This
site is updated regularly. Please use this link to access this list:

http://www.rosenlinks.com/HERO/Jason

FOR FURTHER READING

Apollonius of Rhodes. *Jason and the Argonauts*. Trans. Aaron Poochigian Apollonius. Intro. and notes by Benjamin Acosta-Hughes. New York: Penguin, 2014.

Colavito, Jason. *Jason and the Argonauts Through the Ages*. Jefferson, NC: McFarland & Company, 2014.

Colum, Padraic. *The Golden Fleece and the Heroes Who Lived Before Achilles* (Looking Glass Library). Intro. by Rick Riordan. New York: Random House, 2010.

D'Amato, Raffaele & Andrea Salimbeti. *Bronze Age Greek Warrior 1600–1100 BC*. Oxford: Osprey Publishing, 2011.

Diodorus Siculus. *Library of History. Volume II. Books 2.35–4.58*. Trans. C. H. Oldfather. New York: Harvard University Press, 2006

Euripides. *Medea and Other Plays*. Trans. James Morwood. Oxford: Oxford University Press, 2009.

Gunderson, Jessica. *Jason and the Argonauts* (Greek Myths). North Mankato, MN: Capstone, 2011.

Hawthorne, Nathaniel. *A Wonder Book: Heroes and Monsters of Greek Mythology* (Dover Children's Evergreen Classics). Mineola, NY: Dover Publications, 2012.

Hyde, Natalie. *Understanding Greek Myths* (Myths Understood). New York: Crabtree Publishing, 2012.

Jeffrey, Gary. *Jason and the Argonauts* (Graphic Mythical Heroes). New York: Gareth Stevens Publishing, 2012.

Kuhtz, Cleo & Hazel Mary Martell. *Ancient Greek Civilization* (Ancient Civilizations and Their Myths and Legends). New York: Rosen Publishing Group, 2009.

Nardo, Don. *The Epics of Greek Mythology* (Ancient Greek Mythology). North Mankato, MN: Capstone, 2011.

Nardo, Don. *Medea* (Literary Companion Series). Farmington Hills, MI: Greenhaven, 2000.

Payment, Simone. *Greek Mythology* (Mythology Around the World). New York: Rosen Publishing Group, 2006.

Shelmerdine, Cynthia W., ed. *The Cambridge Companion to the Aegean Bronze Age*. New York: Cambridge University Press, 2008.

Taft, Michael, ed. *Greek Gods & Goddesses* (Gods and Goddesses of Mythology). New York: Britannica Educational Publishing, 2014.

Whiting, Jim. *Jason* (Profiles in Greek & Roman Mythology). Newark, DE: Mitchell Lane, 2007.

INDEX